Verbal Interaction and Development in Families with Adolescents

Advances in Applied Developmental Psychology

Irving E. Sigel, Series Editor

Verbal Interaction and Development in Families with Adolescents

edited by
Manfred Hofer,
James Youniss,
and Peter Noack

Volume 15 in Advances in Applied Developmental Psychology

Ablex Publishing Corporation
Stamford, Connecticut
London, England

Printed in the United States of America

Library of Congress Cataloging-in-Publication Data

Verbal interaction and development in families with adolescents /
  edited by Manfred Hofer, James Youniss, Peter Noack.
    p.   cm. — (Advances in applied developmental psychology ; v.
15)
    Includes bibliographical references (p. 143) and index.
    ISBN 1-56750-391-8 (cloth). — ISBN 1-56750-392-6 (pbk.)
    1. Parent and teenager.   2. Interpersonal relations in
adolescence.   3. Identity (Psychology) in youth.   I. Hofer,
Manfred.   II. Youniss, James.   III. Noack, Peter.   IV. Series:
Advances in applied developmental psychology (1998) ; v. 15.
HQ799. 15.V47   1998
306.874—dc21   98-5760
                                                                    CIP

Ablex Publishing Corporation   Published in the U.K. and Europe by:
100 Prospect Street   Ablex Publishing Corp. (UK)
Stamford, Connecticut 06901-1604   38 Tavistock Street
                                      Covent Garden
                                      London WC2E 7PB
                                      England

Contents

Acknowledgments

The idea for this volume was raised at an international conference on family interaction and adolescent development held at the Werner Reimers Foundation in Bad Homburg, Germany, in June, 1996. This meeting brought together a small group of North American and European scholars from the fields of psychology, sociology, and education. A mix of theoretical and empirical approaches that were represented resulted in vivid discussions and respectful critiques. The chapters of this volume have grown out of this exchange. They are selectively focused on the dynamics of parent–adolescent interactions and deal exclusively with families from Germany and The Netherlands.

We appreciate the support of the German Research Foundation which made possible the conference in Bad Homburg. Secretarial work was done efficiently by Birgit Rebennack. Mary Jo Pugh was able to bring the manuscripts to a form that is readable for an English-speaking audience. Finally, Carmen Himmeroeder-Schmidt has to be mentioned for organizing what sometimes came close to entropy during the last phase of preparing this edited volume.

—Manfred Hofer
James Youniss
Peter Noack
Mannheim, Washington DC, Jena, November, 1997

List of Contributors

Heike Buhl, Department of Psychology, University of Jena, Am Steiger 3/1, D-07743 Jena

Maja Deković, Department of Youth, Family and Life Course; Faculty of Social Sciences; University of Utrecht; Heidelberglaan 2; NL-3584 CS Utrecht

Manfred Hofer, Department of Education, University of Mannheim, Schloss, D-68131 Mannheim

Baerbel Kracke, Department of Education, University of Mannheim, Schloss, D-68131 Mannheim

Lothar Krappmann, Max-Planck Institute for Human Development, Lentzeallee 94, D-14195 Berlin

Kurt Kreppner, Max-Planck Institute for Human Development, Lentzeallee 94, D-14195 Berlin

Jeffrey A. McLellan, Life Cycle Institute, Catholic University of America, Washington, DC 20064

Peter Noack, Department of Psychology, University of Jena, Am Steiger 3/1, D-07743 Jena

Marc Noom, Department of Youth, Family and Life Course; Faculty of Social Sciences; University of Utrecht; Heidelberglaan 2; NL-3584 CS Utrecht

Hans Oswald, Department of Education, University of Potsdam, P.O. Box 60 15 53, D-14415 Potsdam

Beate Schuster, Department of Education, University of Potsdam, P.O. Box 60 15 53, D-14415 Potsdam

Manuela Ullrich, Max-Planck Institute for Human Development, Lentzeallee 94, D-14195 Berlin

Elke Wild, Department of Education, University of Mannheim, Schloss, D-68131 Mannheim

Miranda Yates, Menninger Foundation, Box 829, Topeka, Kansas

James Youniss, Life Cycle Institute, Catholic University of America, Washington, DC 20064

Preface

Irving E. Sigel

This unique volume of research is dedicated to the study of adolescent–parent relationships from an individuation theory conceptual framework, primarily among German families. The uniqueness is particularly evident in the way in which the editors (Hofer, Youniss, and Noack) have organized the volume. Individualistic theory has its roots in the belief that it is a major developmental task for adolescents to establish their identity while simultaneously maintaining a relationship with their parents. This belief or value that is so intrinsic to the Western sense of development has been converted into scientific theory with an array of creative observational and experimental methodologies.

Building on the individuation paradigm, the researchers have zeroed in on discourse as a critical mechanism through which family members interact with one another. The types of discourse reveal how adolescents and their parents differentiate themselves, while still maintaining good relationships with each other. Of course, the authors recognize that other societal institutions such as school and church, as well such subtler cultural forces as the media and social norms of the community, play a part in this complex socialization process.

The set of extra familial social forces that contribute to the dynamic process of individuation and differentiation is alluded to in the McLellan and Yates chapter. Interestingly, this developmental move from differentiation to establish one's identity is also accompanied by integration of the new perspectives arrived at by parents and their adolescent children. This process has the earmarks of a social dialectic in the service of development. The editors, while aware of the embeddedness of the individuation process in the larger socio-cultural context, have skillfully organized samples of their work within the family, which are central to testing the individuation theory.

The studies investigate dyadic and triadic interactions, focusing on the communication patterns among the participants as they engage in tasks provided by the experimenter. These tasks have the potential for involving each of the participants. For example, the participants are asked to plan a three-week family vacation while the investigators observe and record the entire planning process, noting dimensions such as social control and discourse patterns. The interactions in this context form the prime data source for capturing family dynamics in family decision making.

Whatever the instrumentation used, the behaviors observed were in quasi-experimental contexts or in classically arranged experiments. The diversity in location and in methodology allows for a multifaceted approach to the investigation if one were to consider all of the studies to be expressions of the common theory.

The data obtained in these studies were complex in the context of the family interaction paradigm. Each of the authors has presented solid data analyses by sophisticated and elegant quantitative methods. The data are most often behavioral descriptions of discourse. The investigators have devised a number of observational category systems that seem to capture particulars in the discourses which are presumed to be sufficient to test the particular hypotheses set forth. Even though each study particularizes a topic within the broad domain of individuation, the reader can come to an understanding of the issues involved by generating a second level of abstraction, thus arriving at a set of generalizations. The last chapter, by McLellan and Yates, provides such an integration. In fact, the first chapter, by Hofer, Youniss, and Noack, sets the stage for the empirical studies, with the last chapter extending the ramification of the research for broader social understanding. This final chapter rounds out the volume, revealing the broader social significance of the research.

These studies have a unique place in the literature of social development in the family context, especially when one realizes that these studies were done primarily in Germany, a culture with a history consistently stereotyped as being authoritarian when it comes to the family. What these studies reflect is a different Germany, far distant from the era of the Nazis. Also, these studies were done after German unification. Germany is no longer divided between a Western capitalist society with a free market economy, and a rigid, authoritarian communist society, the Deutsches Demokratische Republik (DDR). It now has a blended society after the integration of a social system in which the individuation value was probably antithetical to the Communist ideology. It will be interesting to observe how the individuation theory will fare with the remnants of the DDR regime needing to adapt to the democratic orientation of the modern German state. Germany provides an interesting backdrop to study social change with a historical framework.

This volume is a valuable addition to the *Applied Developmental Psychology* series because it reflects the international character of developmental research. The influence of the American investigators Grotevant and Cooper, as well as Youniss, exemplifies this internationalism and will hopefully bring the European German and Dutch research to the attention of American investigators, revealing shared internationalism. Such sharing enriches the knowledge base for American scholar.

Chapter 1

Introduction

Manfred Hofer
University of Mannheim

James Youniss
Catholic University of America

Peter Noack
University of Jena

VERBAL INTERACTION AND DEVELOPMENT IN FAMILIES WITH ADOLESCENTS

Research on adolescents' discourse with parents has gained wide attention among researchers and theorists. From a social constructivist viewpoint, verbal interaction is a key process in knowledge acquisition and the formation of interpersonal relationships. Participants in interactions affect each other as they negotiate specific content through the normal exchange of ideas. From this perspective, individuals are seen as developing new concepts by actively employing language, gestures, and other cultural tools. Through these same interactions, individuals also construct relationships and roles which then become continuing repositories for shared knowledge and understandings of reality.

Despite the importance of interactions for developmental theory, the analysis of verbal exchange is not yet an established research paradigm. Researchers have more often used self-report measures and questionnaire data. They have also used interview formats to gain insight into the inner worlds of growing persons. These methods are very useful and although each has limitations, their results have been surprisingly compatible and mutually informative. At the same time, such methods can go only so far in uncovering actual processes that parents and adolescents utilize to negotiate and transform their relationship. Focus on verbal behavior in developmental psychology is more common in the study of infants or young children and their mothers and in the study of language acquisition. Since the 1980s, however, research on discourse with older children or adolescents and their parents has emerged as a specialized topic with fruitful results (see Grotevant & Cooper, 1983).

INDIVIDUATION THEORY AS A FRAME IN DEALING WITH THE ADOLESCENT–PARENT RELATIONSHIP

The adolescent–parent relationship, which is the focus of this volume, can be regarded as a prototypical situation for the study of discourse. One resulting line of work has been stimulated by conceptions of individuation, a process by which adolescents establish their individuality while they retain, but alter, their relationship with parents. Individuation theory regards family relationships as changing in character during the course of adolescence. Specifically, adolescents differentiate themselves as distinct persons while they remain open to parental advice and seek parental endorsement. The asymmetry and complementarity of early parent–child relationships are changed continually toward greater reciprocity, mutuality, and equality.

Verbal interaction, which at any moment expresses the underlying structure of this relationship, is also used by the partners as a means to renegotiate their relationship and roles. Parents try to adapt to the new demands and needs of the growing adolescent while adolescents alter their orientations to parental authority and distribution of responsibility. During this transformation, parents' and adolescents' interactions are characterized by conflict as well as by intimate closeness. Regardless of the kind of emphasis at any moment, interactions are an analytic tool that give insights into the ways participants confirm and transform their relationship.

In this theory, individuality does not mean individualism. Adolescents and the adult persons they are becoming are also members of relationships in which the parties are responsible to and respectful of one another. It follows, then, that the unilateral exercise of authority which satisfied the demands of childhood must be transformed into greater equality in which parents and adolescents acknowledge one another's competence and recognize their mutual dependence in their relationship.

This concept was developed mainly in studies of families in the United States and is, to some degree, a reflection of social–political context that is characteristic of American culture. From cross-cultural research in general, it is clear that culture conditions the determinants and consequences of education and development. This would seem evident for ways in which families manage their interactions, deal with goals, and address their conflicts. The concept of individuation is clearly applicable to modern societies that are structured on the premise that strong individuals know and can represent their own interests. In recent treatments of the history of adolescence in the United States (Kett, 1971) and western Europe (Gillis, 1981), the family has receded as the primary source of identity as individuals in successive generations have constructed adult lives that do not depend on their forbears' status or social position. This understanding of the individual was taken to extremes, however, especially in functionalist accounts of sociology during the 1950s and 1960s. It failed to recognize the degree to which individuals still relied on families and networks of kin and acquaintances in their daily intercourse of work, recreation, and community functioning. So, a more balanced view evolved to take account of the dual reality of separateness and connectedness.

FAMILY INTERACTION IN EUROPE

This conception, which seems to fit so well with America's mixture of individual freedom and communitarianism, clashes with the stereotype of the German authoritarian family. That stereotype was advanced after World War II to explain the sordid events under the Nazi regime. The stereotype repeated in the works of Adorno and his colleagues, Eric Fromm and Gordon Allport. As empirical results show, there was some truth in it. In the 1950s, physical punishment, threat and arrest were commonly accepted by Germans as adequate sanctions in conflict situations. This is consistent considering their preferences for obedience, order, and diligence as important educational goals. Children tended to react with consent and direct or indirect resistance (Fischer, Fuchs, & Zinnecker, 1985). This is what one might have expected from the results of the early studies on experimentally created social climates by Lewin, Lippitt, and White (1939).

In the 1960s, a general mistrust of adolescents against their parents' generation can be regarded as one of the causes of the so-called student movement. It consisted of a mixture of cultural revolution and pacifism. The old idea of renewal of societal structures by the next generation got new meaning. Reforms of educational practices and institutions were of central concern and gave rise to the anti-authoritarian movement. Competition and exploitation were considered main sources of individual alienation. A second element was the rejection of patriotic values like nation, authority, and defense of national interest against threats from outside. Instead, freedom, autonomy, solidarity, and peace were introduced as new societal goals. These ideas were proposed mainly by college students who at that time did not exceed five percent of the youth generation. But they were shared by many of the youth (Kreutz, 1974). Most of the older generation rejected the reforms proposed. Thus, the relationship between the generations in the late 1960s and early 1970s indeed resembled the constellation of a classical generation conflict.

The student revolution was very influential on German society as well as on most western European countries and had a large impact especially in the field of education. Fundamental reforms in the school system were initiated. Starting from the early 1970s, educational values and practices also became more liberal. For example, educational aims in the German population shifted heavily toward more autonomy and less obedience in the 1980s. Educational practices within families generally became less strict in control and gained in emotionality. Adolescents became more self-reliant; they decided about matters of their personal jurisdiction, and began to participate in family decisions. Adolescent–parent relations got tighter; mutual respect rose (Oswald, 1980).

As a consequence, the stereotype of the authoritarian German family appears limp and unfounded in current German family life. Indeed, German youth are no more intolerant or authoritarian in their outlook than youth in other countries such as the United States. A cross-cultural study considering youth cohorts from the early post-war years until the late 1970s (Lederer, 1983) illustrates marked changes in authoritarianism among young west Germans. While the first data clearly confirm the expectation of the adherence to authoritarian ideas in Germany, the consecutive assessments suggest a decline resulting in parallel findings for young North Americans and Germans. A more recent comparison conducted in 1990–1991 including 16-year-olds from West Germany, the German Democratic Republic, and the U.S. (Ripple & Boehnke, 1995) yielded little general variation. Focusing on parental authority, west German teenagers showed less acceptance of authoritarianism than their east German agemates while young Americans ranged somewhere in between. Taking a different theoretical point of departure, Wilder (1995) examined unilateral authority and mutuality of parent–adolescent relations in U.S. and west German families. Again, little culture-specific variation was observed except for negligibly higher levels of unilateralness in the U.S. sample.

Changes in the German family system can be summarized by shifts from a command family toward a discourse family (Fischer, Fuchs, & Zinnecker, 1985). An important change in the relation concerns the mode of interaction. Negotiation became the principal mode of dealing with conflictual goals. Education, which rests on order and obedience, does not leave much room for verbal interaction, arguments, and negotiation. Adolescents learned to employ verbal means such as persuasion, attempts to convince, arguments, compromise, or flattery in order to influence their parents. At the same time, parents had to change their strategies and also start compromising with, persuading, and convincing their kids, as commands are not regarded as adequate educational practice anymore. As Habermas' work (1981) shows, ideas of communicative action, of ideal discourse, and of egalitarian relationships found considerable attention in philosophy as well.

Researchers interested in family and adolescent development realized this new socialization climate and became interested in concepts apt to describe the relationships in development. They turned toward the work of authors like Kohlberg, Damon, Selman, and Youniss (e.g., in Edelstein & Keller, 1982). They initiated research and made use of the ideas introduced above, finding that individuation theoretic concepts are useful in describing and explaining adolescent–parent relationships in Germany also.

We may be observing the manifestation of an association between the social democratic structures of the larger context and family relations. A fundamental question is why any parent cohort would adopt one or the other approach to the rearing of their adolescent offspring. The answer could be that parents are seeking what is best for adolescents by preparing them and providing an orientation for the society which they are about to enter as adults. Hence, in the western European countries which—with a grain of salt—could be well described in terms of social democratic societies, granting autonomy while remaining connected seems to be an apt parental strategy. Goals and practices of socialization guiding the concept of individuation can provide a sound basis for young people's future.

It is open to question, however, whether we are presently seeing the end of the welfare state in Europe. Starting with the collapse of the East bloc, eastern European societies are not the only countries facing dramatic transformations. The growing internationalization of markets and communication, economic stagnation or even recession, and unforeseen changes of the geopolitical landscape are but a few instances of new challenges casting doubt on the successful adherence to traditional political and economic responses. While the U.S. is often cited as a promising example of how to take on the demands of the future, several European countries seem uncertain how to move forward. Germany, in particular, looks almost paralyzed at present. The immediate economic boost after unification had postponed the necessary adjustments which are now on the agenda as Germany faces massive financial burdens as a result of the unification.

Attacks against foreigners, burning homes of asylum seekers, and similar incidents for some look like a return to authoritarian rule in Germany as a response to economic strain and swift social change. Even though violent action is limited to very small factions of the German society, it is unclear to what extent the everyday lives of the majority of the population, and thus typical modes of socialization, may also be affected by the ongoing societal transformations. It seems plausible to assume new intergenerational conflicts will arise. Using individuation theoretical terminology, one could expect young people to strive for individuality without regard for socio-emotional bonds with their parents and that this will be a basis for the transformation of family relations. Likewise, adolescents may be trapped in the warm security of strong connectedness with their fathers and mothers and fear the challenges of growing autonomy in the increasingly demanding adult world. There has been little empirical research addressing this issue. The few findings presently available (e.g., Hofer & Puschner, 1997; Noack, Oepke, & Sassenberg, in press) are far from being conclusive. There are indications of growing connectedness, but also more authoritarian parenting practices in response to the swift social change. In any case, applying notions of individuation theory to the situation of present-day Germany and other European country promises insights fruitful for the development of the theory as well as for the understanding of adolescent socialization in the family unit in modern societies.

THE RESEARCH PRESENTED IN THIS VOLUME

The present volume offers examples of studies of western European families undertaken by western European researchers. These researchers view the concept of individuation as a meaningful tool for what they believe to be normative in the development of relationships and verbal interactions in families in Germany and the Netherlands. The individual studies show how these researchers approached the concept methodologically, and the studies report data that enrich the concept through new empirical instances. On the one hand, these studies replicate findings on families in the United States and, thus, offer a test of their generalizability across cultures. On the other hand, these studies offer new ways of parsing interactive exchanges and report new results that go beyond replication. In this regard, the present work adds to the state of our knowledge by affording fresh perspectives from a new cultural setting.

The chapters may be viewed from a methodological perspective as offering samples of three broad approaches. At one extreme, an interpretative description of parent–adolescent negotiation is used to categorize ways in which mothers and daughters deal with their changing relationships. At the other extreme, an experimental approach was used to manipulate hypothetical states of adolescent–parent relations to which subjects then constructed appropriate responses. In the middle are studies in which interactions are audio- or videotaped, then coded into category systems which were submitted for statistical analysis. We offer these diverse approaches not so much for contrast, as to show their complementary and synergistic value.

The chapters also deal with the question of whether discourse is consistent over situations and stable over time. Cross-situational stability and temporal continuity of verbal behavior can be regarded as fundamental prerequisites for the usefulness of these variables in research. On the other hand, empirical results on these matters can shed light on the function of interactions in the process of parent–adolescent relationships. Situations between adolescents and parents may involve different challenges for the partners, and those situations have to be dealt with in different ways. On the other hand, in the conception of transformation of relationship, interactions may vary over time, depending on the development of the relationship.

Finally, the chapters are devoted to determinants and consequences of verbal interactions. The way parents and adolescents exchange meanings may change according to variations across kinds of persons or relations. Families which differ in the degree of cohesion and adaptability (see Olson & Lavee, 1989) can differ systematically in their interactions. And what might be normal in "normal" families can be different in adoptive families. Within an individuation theoretic line of thinking the question concerning the effects of specific interaction patterns on individual development arises. If interactions are means of transforming relationships, they should be related to the psychosocial functioning of the individuals involved. Especially, the successful transformation of relationships should foster the development of autonomy in the adolescents and, as a consequence, also contribute to their overall psychosocial adjustment.

According to the types of questions raised, the book is organized into three parts. This first chapter describes the goals of this volume, the scope of the research, and its relevance to the literature on adolescence, families, and parent–adolescent relationships. The following chapter by Lothar Krappmann, Hans Oswald, Beate Schuster, and James Youniss, "Can mothers win?—The transformation of mother–daughter relationships in late childhood," offers an example of an interpretative analysis of videotaped interactions. The power of the approach lies in its ability to identify subtle strategies that mothers and daughters use to negotiate their varying and changing views of authority. At the other extreme, Heike Buhl and Manfred Hofer in "Experiments with the role-playing method in the study of interactive behavior," present an example of the experimental method employed to analyze antecedents of daughters' interactive behavior in conflicts with their mothers. In this study, adolescent respondents generate appropriate behaviors for standard instances within their cognitive repertoire of relational possibilities.

The studies presented in the second section of the book address both substantive and methodological issues. In "Relationship and family discourse in different situations," Manfred Hofer and Kai Sassenberg examine the cross-situational stability of interactive behavior and find high correspondences despite the fact that different tasks had to be accomplished and different coding systems were applied in the two types of discourse studied. Peter Noack and Baerbel Kracke analyze the temporal stability of interactional behavior in their chapter "Continuity and change in family interactions across adolescence." The results are based on two longitudinal studies of families with early and late adolescents, thus informing the changes from asymmetric to more symmetric interaction patterns.

Chapters 6 to 8 investigate individual and family differences that produce variations in individuation. In "Talk to mom and dad and listen to what is in between," Kurt Kreppner and Manuela Ullrich identified different styles of communication which are linked to three types of relationship qualities as assessed by adolescents self-reports in a longitudinal design. Also, the role of parental communication patterns in discussions with each other for adolescents' differential experiences are addressed. Marc Noom and Maja Deković, in "Family interaction as a context for the development of adolescent autonomy," address the question whether specific interaction styles of parents are related to aspects of autonomy of their adolescents. Finally, in "Family interaction and psychosocial adjustment of adopted and nonadopted adolescents," Elke Wild looks at the influence of adoption on parent–adolescent interactions. She compares adopted with nonadopted adolescents' social adjustment insofar as it is associated with patterned variations in parent–adolescent verbal interactions. The perspective of self-determination theory nicely fits in the individuation theoretic notions referred to in the other chapters of the book. The studies reported in all three chapters used different systems to code verbal behavior and analyzed correspondences between questionnaire data and behavior in interactions. Thus, they add to our knowledge about the objective and the subjective aspects of communication.

The last chapter by Jeffrey McLellan and Miranda Yates is a commentary on the contributions of the book. It provides evaluative reflections on each chapter and identifies themes that merit special consideration. They focus on methodological variations, theoretical contributions, and point to issues worth pursuing in future research.

Each chapter of this book can be regarded as a variation on the theme of adolescents gaining autonomy while they preserve connectedness. This task, which is important for any enduring relationship, is central for parents and their adolescent sons and daughters. The traditional theme of "storm and stress" no longer adequately describes the character of parent–adolescent relationship. For present purposes, individuation theory provides a more fruitful framework for understanding the dynamics of this relationship. It stresses the fact that in many contemporary societies, adolescents must become individuals with the competence to function outside parental support and supervision.

REFERENCES

Edelstein, W. & Keller, M. (1982). *Perspektivität und Interpretation* [Perspective and interpretation]. Frankfurt: Suhrkamp.

Fischer, A., Fuchs, W, & Zinnecker, J. (Eds.). (1985). *Jugendliche und Erwachsene '85. Generationen im Vergleich. Band 3* [Youth and adults 1985. Comparing generations]. Opladen, Germany: Leske & Budrich.

Grotevant, H. D., & Cooper, C. R. (Eds.). (1983). *Adolescent Development in the Family.* San Francisco: Jossey-Bass.

Gillis, J. R. (1981). *Youth and History: Tradition and Change in European Age Relations 1770–Present.* New York: Academic Press.

Habermas, J. (1981). *Theorie des kommunikativen Handelns* [Theory of Communicative Action]. Frankfurt: Suhrkamp.

Hofer, M., & Puschner, B. (1997, October). *Beziehungswandel—sozialer Wandel: Analysen der Beziehungen in ost- und westdeutschen Familien mit Jugendlichen nach der Vereinigung* [Relationship change—social change: Analyses of parent–adolescent relationships in east and west German families after unification]. Paper presented at the 55. Tagung der Arbeitsgemeinschaft fuer Empirische Paedagogische Forschung, Berlin, Germany.

Kett, J. (1971). Adolescence and youth in nineteenth century America. *Journal of Interdisciplinary History, 2,* 283–298.

Kreutz, H. (1974). *Soziologie der Jugend* [Sociology of Youth]. Muenchen, Germany: Juventa.

Lederer, G. (1983). *Jugend und Autoritaet.* [Youth and Authority]. Opladen, Germany: Westdeutscher Verlag.

Lewin, K., Lippitt, R., & White, R. K. (1939). Patterns of aggressive behavior in experimentally created "social climates." Journal of Social Psychology, 10, 271–299.

Noack, P., Oepke, M., & Sassenberg, K. (in press). Individuation in ost- und westdeutschen Familien und Erfahrungen sozialen Wandels. [Individuation in east and west German families and experiences of social change]. *Zeitschrift fuer Sozialisationsforschung und Erziehungssoziologie.*

Olson, D. H., & Lavee, Y. (1989). Family systems and family stress: A family life cycle perspective. In K. Kreppner & R. M. Lerner (Eds.), *Family Systems and Life-Span Development* (pp. 165–195). Hillsdale, NJ: Erlbaum.

Oswald, H. (1980). *Abdankung der Eltern? Eine empirische Untersuchung ueber den Einfluss von Eltern auf Gymnasiasten* [Resignation of Parents? An Empirical Investigation on Parental Influence on High-Track Highschool Students]. Weinheim, Germany: Beltz.

Ripple, S., & Boehnke, K. (1995). Authoritarianism: Adolescents from east and west Germany and the United States compared. In J. Youniss (Ed.), *After the Wall: Family Adaptations in East and West Germany.* San Francisco: Jossey-Bass.

Wilder, D. (1995). *Changes in Relationship Closeness, Reciprocity, and Authority During Adolescence.* Unpublished Master's thesis, Florida Atlantic University.

Chapter 2

Can Mothers Win?
The Transformation of Mother–Daughter
Relationships in Late Childhood

Lothar Krappmann
Max-Planck Institute for Human Development

Beate Schuster
University of Potsdam

James Youniss
Catholic University of America

GENERAL PROBLEM

The question "Can mothers win?" does not seem to make sense. Why should mothers not be able to win a game they play with their very young or preadolescent daughters? Our observations of mothers and daughters have revealed that the problem is more complicated than it first appears. Winning a game requires keeping rules that guarantee each partner of a game the same chance to win. Play partners are equals with regard to their joint activities. Can mothers and daughters be equals?

Piaget (1926/1971) and Sullivan (1953/1983) stated that children's relationships to parents and peers differ structurally. The parent–child relationship is structured according to the principle of unilateral authority which assigns parents to a position of authority, and children must operate in complement. In children's relationships to peers and friends, however, children expect that both partners control the interaction. This thesis was elaborated by Youniss (1980) and corroborated by a number of studies which have shown that children apply different procedures and rules when they interact with parents or same-aged children (e.g., Bigelow, Tesson, & Lewko, 1996; Kruger & Tomasello, 1986; Youniss & Smollar, 1985).

Young children certainly are dependent on parental support when they are confronted with not yet schematized, incomprehensible, and unpredictable reactions and behaviors of objects and persons. When children, however, begin to be aware of persons' differing interpretations of meanings and norms (Hoppe-Graff & Keller, 1988; Selman, 1980), they also begin to demand more respect of their views and intentions from their parents (Vuchinich, Angelelli, & Gatherum, 1996). These requests may cause serious conflicts which can be solved by development of autonomy based either on separation from parents or by reshaping the parent–child relationship in terms of a more egalitarian exchange.

The latter alternative, development of autonomy by a transformation of the unilateral parent–child relationship to a more egalitarian relationship, received broader recognition in recent years. Already Piaget (1926/1971) mentioned that a more egalitarian type of interaction between adults and children may emerge when adults try to restrain the influence of their superior expertise and competence on adult–child interaction. Although children and adolescents usually describe the unilateral structure of the parent–child relationship in a consistent manner (Youniss & Smollar, 1985), family-interaction research demonstrates that already in middle childhood (for reviews see Duck, 1993; Parke & Kellam, 1994) this basic structure is enacted in various ways. Also parenting research shows that many parents wish to raise their children in a way that fosters autonomy, responsibility, and self-confidence (Bronfenbrenner, 1985; Martin, Halverson, Olsen, Pesce-Trudell, & Dumka, 1993; Schneewind, 1996).

Most parents claim that they are willing to negotiate dissent with their children and no longer simply forbid or ask for strict obedience. Yet parents often have a hard time when their children intensely begin to demand respect of their own issues, problems, and plans which result from their involvement in school and peer world. Teachers, classmates, and friends expect from children of this age that they will keep to the agreements made. Therefore, children confront their parents with obligations and arrangements which cannot be easily changed. They also want to be regarded as persons who can competently negotiate and decide on matters which belong to their domains of life. Negotiation with parents also achieves a new quality as children have acquired more effective strategies which enable them to promote their intentions (Cooper & Carlson, 1991; Grotevant & Cooper, 1985; Hofer & Pikowsky, 1993; Kobak, Cole, Ferenz-Gillies, & Fleming, 1993).

As girls mature earlier than boys, the mother–daughter relationship may be challenged by emerging demands for respect and autonomy earlier and more clearly than the mother–son relationship (Steinberg & Silverberg, 1986). Girls' request for more respect may also cause more serious conflicts than the respective request of boys, because still today many parents expect more social adjustment from girls than from boys. Research has demonstrated that girls are especially dependent on their mothers' sensitive understanding, support, and closeness (Du Bois-Reymond & Ravesloot,1995; Simmons & Blyth, 1987) when they are confronted with the critical task of redefining their social and subjective self-definitions (Alsaker, 1995; Fend, 1994). Do mothers offer this kind of supportive understanding? Mothers are exposed to multifaceted demands in the interaction system of the family. Mostly they are addressed when children need support (Dekovic, 1991), and they feel especially responsible for the harmony of the family (Vuchinich, 1987). Therefore, they try to avoid conflict and reduce tensions. This situation may be responsible for the observed fact that mothers send more affectively mixed messages to their maturing daughters than to their sons (Flannery, Montemayor, Eberly, & Torquati, 1993). These findings suggest that it may not be easy for mothers to manifest the kind of understanding needed by daughters.

In this chapter we intend to demonstrate that daughters and mothers begin to renegotiate their relationship already in late childhood and preadolescence. As daughters primarily are concerned about their position in the mother–daughter relationship, the analyses focus on the strategies applied by daughters in order to achieve a more egalitarian relationship. Since we do not want to examine which strategies are mostly used or to which other variables the strategies applied are related, we choose six mother–daughter dyads from a larger sample which most clearly illustrate the variety of strategies and patterns observed in the total sample.

Three questions will be studied:

1. In which ways do mothers try to exert unilateral control?
2. How do daughters react to those maternal attempts and which strategies do they apply to achieve more respect for their perspective?
3. Which interaction patterns emerge as mothers and daughters make accommodations for one another?

METHOD

In order to study the qualities of mother–child interactions, we created a situation that urges both parents and children to interact in an egalitarian and reciprocal manner. A game of the "plan something together" type (Grotevant & Carlson, 1987) was designed which subjected mothers and their children to the same set of rules and stimulated competition for winning the game. Since parents may tend to give up their authority in play situations without striving to win, some issues which should excite dissension were added to the game. These issues were designed to make mothers concerned about their daughters' behaviors (Schuster, 1997). The potential conflicts should reveal whether mothers are willing to give up their parental authority in such a play situation or try to maintain control over the situation in a way not shared with the child. They also should show how children react to these parental attempts of control.

Six dyads of mothers and daughters, who were between 9 and 13 years old, were selected from the total sample (50 dyads, daughters age between 7 and 13 years) to provide clear illustrations of the conflicts which accompany the transformation process of the parent–child relationship and of the variety of strategies by which girls react to their mothers' suggestions and demands. The children attended an inner-city primary school (2nd to 5th grade) located in a middle-class to lower-class neighborhood of Berlin, Germany.

During the sessions, mothers and children were seated at a table on which a game board was placed. The game required that they imagine they were on a vacation trip and had to decide how to spend time together. The board depicted 10 activities that were to be chosen one at a time, in sequence. Five of the activities were child-oriented and five were adult-oriented. The child activities were rather fun and consumer-oriented (an action movie, a video game hall, a fast food restaurant, swimming, and pony-riding) whereas the mothers' activities were cultural sites or things typically liked by adults but not by children (visiting an old cathedral, a museum for antique art, a sightseeing tour by bus, hiking in the woods, eating in an expensive seafood restaurant). For each activity, the players had to pay a fixed amount of money, ranging from $3 for visiting the old cathedral to $20 for the seafood restaurant (e.g., mothers were given $200 in play bills to pay for all activities, whereas the child got some pocket money only ($15 in play bills) sufficient for one or two activities). The general rules of the game were: When a child convinced the mother to give money for a child activity (or when she uses her pocket money), the child earned positive points, and the mother earned negative points. The reverse was true when a mother persuaded her child to join her in one of the adult activities. She earned positive points and the daughter negative ones. The players depended on each other and had to negotiate their differing interests. The exact means for getting the other to go along with one's wishes was left to the players. The average time of playing the game was about 18 minutes.

A hermeneutic approach was chosen in order to understand the meaning of actions from the perspectives of both, the mother and the daughter. The main goal was to get insight into the ways in which mothers and daughters try to realize their understanding of the mother–daughter relationship. We are talking of strategies because we want to underline that mothers and daughters are goal-oriented when they propose, disprove, contradict, or react to one another. We were less interested in the players' efforts to win the game than in their attempts to define the quality of their relationship. Interpretations were regarded as hypotheses which were repeatedly tested with regard to whether they can make understandable the contributions of partners to the interaction process.

RESULTS

Mothers' Methods of Exerting Unilateral Control

Each mother of the six dyads selected was apparently affected by the idea that a game generates an egalitarian situation which should offer the same rights and opportunities to both partners. Mothers' behaviors showed that they were aware of the inadequateness of behaviors by which they control the situation in a unilateral manner. All but one, however, severely struggled with the definitions of situation and relationship which were suggested by their daughters' actions and reactions. Still, they all tried to maintain a satisfying and intimate relationship with their daughters. Though they dealt with the problem in different ways, they fundamentally did not give up their authoritative roles.

The mother of dyad 4 seemed to be untouched by the problem of renegotiating the relationship. This mother was interested in the game and behaved in a rational and emotionally cold way toward her daughter. Great distance was generated in the relationship by this attitude. She did not take notice of her daughter's wishes; she only viewed the situation from her own perspective. Since she somehow treated her daughter like an adult, she may have thought they had an egalitarian partnership. Yet she, of all the mothers, was least aware that the perspective of her daughter was different because she simply imputed the same rational adult perspective to her daughter which she herself followed. She was not at all sensitive to the actual feeling and understanding of her daughter.

The attitudes of two mothers were characterized by relatively balanced emotional concern. They differed according to the clarity by which they expressed their demands on their daughters. The mother of dyad 6 was emotionally open and self-confident but had very rigid demands while, in contrast, the mother of dyad 5 admitted that her daughter unrestrictedly used her opportunities, but did not reveal her own expectations and submitted herself to the daughter's suggestions without a clarifying comment.

Thus, on the one hand, both mothers were emotionally accessible, but on the other hand, the daughter of dyad 5 got no orientation at all about her mother's goals, and the daughter of dyad 6 was confronted with fixed demands. In both cases, a negotiation process could not take place.

The mothers of dyads 1 and 2 were distressed by the anticipation of negotiating the relationship with their daughters, although both mothers sensitively understood their daughters' perspective. Thus, they tried to keep the process under unilateral control. The mother of dyad 1 tried to control her daughter by presenting herself as dependent on her daughter's cooperation to the extent that any step to more autonomy would deeply hurt her. The mother of dyad 2 intended to solve the anticipated problem in advance by generously offering her daughter free access to the money. By arranging situations in which daughters could do something in favor of her mother she stimulated the idea of equality between mother and daughter. She even broke the rules of the game in order to prevent negotiations of the relationship because she was afraid to lose her daughter's sympathy when she would actually let her negotiate the relationship. In different ways both mothers failed to cope with their anxiety of separation in a way which would allow for emotional independence of their daughters. Whereas the mother of dyad 1 clearly expressed by her demonstrated vulnerability that she expected her daughter to stay in the complementary role, the mother of dyad 2, who tried by all means to give her daughter the "impression of being an equal partner," sent confusing signals, because she ultimately could not abandon her role as the responsible mother.

The mother of dyad 3 displayed an emotionally balanced attitude and was open to her daughter's understanding of the situation. More than the other mothers, she was willing to encourage her daughter's endeavors of being a successful player. She interpreted her daughter's behaviors not as an egoistic compulsion, but sensitively perceived her daughter's intention to be accepted as an equal partner with the right to contribute her own ideas and proposals. Without giving up her own opinions, this mother was able to flexibly adapt herself to differing demands. At the same time she expected her daughter to respect her demands in the same way and, thus, allowed for an effective negotiation process.

This mother was the only one who succeeded in balancing game interactions and relationship with respect to emotional closeness as well as structural organization—the constitutional dimensions of every social system ("cohesion" and "adaptability" according to Olson, McCubbin, Barnes, Larson, Muxen, & Wilson, 1989). The behaviors within the other five dyads were assigned to the extreme poles of these two dimensions and basically obliterated the negotiation process. Three of these mothers behaved in the extreme with regard to the cohesion dimension. The mothers of dyads 1 and 2 were extremely close to their daughters, giving no chance of separation. Both were assigned on the "high" end of the co-hesion dimension ("enmeshed"), although they were located on oppo-site poles of the structural dimension (the mother of dyad 1 on the "low" end because of her rigidity; the mother of dyad 2 was on the "high" end because of her unclear reactions). Also the mother of dyad 4 held rigid expectations ("low adaptability"); she was at the same time "low" on the cohesion dimension, because she behaved in a cold and "distanced" manner ("low cohesion"). The mothers of dyads 3, 5 and 6 were emotion-ally relatively balanced ("medium cohesion"), but differed according to the flexibility of their expectations, which were rigid in dyad 6 ("low adaptability") and unclear in dyad 5 ("high adaptability"). Except for dyad 3, the mothers' fixations hampered an open exchange which would allow reactions that take into account the perspectives of both mother and daughter. These combinations of behavioral orientations resulted in different kinds of unilateral control.

Thus the daughters had to deal with social processes which were unbal-anced in different ways. Correspondingly they used different strategies to express their dissatisfaction, push their demands, and resist unilateral con-trol.

Daughters' Strategies

These 9- to 13-year-old girls opposed their mothers' unilateral procedures to an unexpected extent and sensitively reacted when they felt misunder-stood by their mothers (e.g., when their mothers presupposed that they only wanted to win the game, or when the daughters blamed their mothers for not being authentic). The behavior of almost all girls expressed that they were aware of their independent selves. Some of them already had clear ideas of how they wanted to be seen by their mothers.

We will now describe and illustrate the groups of strategies observed. For this exposition we will give only one example for each strategy, but other strategies of the same type will be noted.

Cooperate

Children who were cooperating accepted responsibility for maintaining the interaction and successfully playing the game. Cooperation does not imply that the daughter conforms, but that she expresses her ideas, inten-tions, and understanding so that joint actions are based on both partners' expertise and competence. Cooperating daughters behaved respectfully to-ward their mothers and took into account their expectations. However, it was important for them to make clear that they were not acting as inferior participants. Rather they demonstrated that they were capable and reliable partners who contribute to playing on their own. Thus, they did not simply *demand* to be treated in an egalitarian way but *convinced* their mothers of their equal status. These cooperative strategies made sense only with regard to mothers who were sensitive to this kind of interaction in which the preceding mother–daughter relationship is transformed to more egalitarian exchange.

A typical cooperative strategy was *establishing a shared procedure.* Using this strategy, daughters clearly stated their goals and which rules they believed should be observed by both mothers and daughters.

For example, one mother proposed to exclude the electronic games from the tour. The daughter retorted that the cathedral should be skipped also in order to balance the distribution of points. At the same time the daughter accepted her mother's intention of planning "a proper vacation tour," but insisted that the planning initiated by her mother was changed to an egalitarian exchange.

Other strategies which demonstrate daughters' cooperative intentions were *explaining one's own ideas or behaviors* and *giving reasons for agreements or refusals.*

Strike a balance

When mothers were not sensitive to their daughters' efforts of establishing a more egalitarian relationship, they often provoked daughters to use stronger means for gaining recognition. Daughters then challenged, contradicted, and established opposing positions sometimes trickily using mother's procedures against their original intentions. They confronted their mothers with the fact that they were rivals who were not afraid of conflicts. They also appealed to rules which concern mother and daughter in the same way. These strategies were not appropriate to establish egalitarian cooperation. Only symmetrical stalemate could be achieved. Mothers learned that their control capacity was limited. But daughters still could not achieve equality.

One strategy of this type we called *challenging mother.* This strategy was used, for example, when daughters were not willing to submit to their mothers' scene-setting attempts. Daughters purposely destroyed their mother's play inventions by challenging them as the following sequence indicates.

A mother described the attractive exhibits of the museum and added that the daughter's friend certainly would like to join them. Instead of accepting the frame, the daughter challenged her mother's scene-setting by asking: "How do you know what there is in the museum? Did you find this information in the game instruction?" Of course, the daughter knew that no information of this kind was included in the information sheet. Thus, she disclosed her mother's irrelevant fantasy fabrication.

Other strategies that daughters could use to strike the balance were *ignore mother's suggestion, turn the playful argument into a rational context, tit-for-tat,* and *refer to rules and teach the mother.*

Thwarting mother's intentions

A more effective way to gain a more egalitarian position is shown in strategies of thwarting. Thwarting confronts mothers with implications of their procedures which they could not have meant, so that they have to reconsider the appropriateness of their behaviors. Thus, mothers were not confronted with opposing reactions, but with mirrors of their own behaviors. In terms of family-system theory, thwarting provokes "a second order change" (Schneewind, 1995), since this strategy aims at a change of the rules of the relationship system itself and not only of a particular behavior. The usual method of control can no longer be applied as daughters showed that something was wrong at the basis of mothers' attempts. Because daughters did not attack mothers but just revealed unintended consequences of their behaviors, the chance of a co-constructive redefinition of the situation and the relationship is fostered.

Daughters who used thwarting strategies, for instance, may have *ridiculed mother's intention."* They did not only ignore their mothers' suggestions, but demonstrated that mothers' suggestions cannot be taken as serious contributions to the continuation of the game. For instance, when a daughter observed her mother's forced scene-setting efforts, she reacted with a bored facial expression and the ironic comment "How nice!" trying to make a fool out of her mother.

Other strategies that daughters could use to thwart mothers' intentions were *distort mother's scene setting for self gain, accept proposal but devalue,* and *indulgently react to mothers' criticism or reproaches.*

Dominating (turning around the relationship)

While thwarting is a sophisticated strategy of achieving more respect, dominating strategies are a crude means aimed at forcing mothers into an inferior position. Two subgroups of dominating strategies were observed, both of which generated role reversal in the mother–daughter relationship. In some situations daughters in fact knew better what had to be done. However, they exploited the situation to their own advantage by not sharing their knowledge, but used it to humiliate their mother.

The first subgroup of dominating strategies consisted of verbal or nonverbal violence. The second subgroup contained procedures by which daughters addressed problems of their mothers which were embarrassing for them. Both kinds of strategies made mothers helpless, and they often reacted by ignoring. Daughters who used these strategies apparently were not fully aware of the offensive character of their behaviors. Without doubt, these procedures were not solutions for overcoming unilaterality because these behaviors did not create mutual respect and cooperation but forced mothers to withdraw.

The first type of domination includes strategies like commanding, determining, and harassing or behaving without respect and empathy toward their mothers.

The second type comprises procedures like *bring mother into embarrassment.* Another procedure was *excuse and help mother in order to humiliate her.* Humiliating daughters did not support their mothers when mishaps occurred as daughters did who dominated by commanding or harassing. Rather they helped in a way which made mothers look even more silly.

For example, one mother got very irritated when her daughter explained the downfall of the figure which represented the mother in the game, by referring to "a little bit too much wine." The mother was shocked and embarrassed. The daughter used her mother's momentary helplessness to turn the relationship upside down completely as she did not deny the statement rather than declared that she was only joking.

Ingratiating

Some daughters did not question their mothers' authority and avoided negotiating with their mothers as partners in their own right. Instead, they tried to get what they wanted using ingratiating strategies. These daughters did not change the relationship. On the contrary, they confirmed their dependency on their mother's decisions and asked mothers to behave leniently and generously, as mothers do toward little children. By stressing their inferior position, daughters evaded efforts of convincing their mothers by appeals to fairness and justice or to the rules of the game and egalitarian exchange.

Daughters were aware that the unilateral structure of the relationship would advance their interests. However, they were not yet able to address directly the inadequateness of this asymmetry with regard to the present situation. They were trapped into the contradiction between the egalitarian rules of the game and the sustained unilateral mother–daughter relationship.

One form of ingratiating consisted of *behaving in a preventive or compensating way* toward the mother. This behavior was observable when daughters had already achieved a compromise with their mother. Although they were allowed to do something they wanted, they felt the need to please their mothers as if they had demanded too much from them. Conversely mothers displayed feelings of vulnerability or distress and thereby stimulated guilt. Daughters tried to compensate for these impositions.

One daughter, for instance, who had convinced her reluctant mother after long debate to allow video games, invented a scene designed to reduce her mother's unease. She invited her mother to join her by saying: "You can sit down there . . . certainly they have a cup of coffee or something else you like." Although the daughter had skillfully negotiated with her mother, she did not dare to stay in the egalitarian position and reestablished the preceding type of a submissive relationship.

Two other types of this strategy were *behaving babylike in order to push one's interests* and *giving vague hints only at one's intentions*.

Yielding or giving up

Daughters who mainly yield to their mothers' proposals or immediately drop their own suggestions when mothers resist, miss the opportunity to negotiate the unilateral structure of the mother–child relationship. They conform without adding their own deliberations to their mothers' view. Although their mothers sometimes behave in an authoritarian and degrading way, their reactions reveal that they are used to submitting to their mothers' expectations and regulations. Mothers define the situation and their daughters go along with it.

While daughters using ingratiating strategies still want their mothers to satisfy their wishes, yielding daughters refuse to shape the situation. They fail to introduce their own element into the interaction. There was rarely a hint indicating that daughters would like to share more responsibility. Mostly these girls had given up attempts to be more respected by their mothers. Frustration appeared in their facial expression, demonstrating that their passivity was not a consequence of agreement with the mothers but rather a strategy of avoiding further disapproval. Yielding strategies are not completely profitable for mothers; the strategies put pressure on the mothers as they alone become responsible for playing the game successfully.

Two ways of yielding were observed: *No pursuit of own intentions* and *immediate accommodation*. One daughter, for instance, who was asked not to play the video games, enumerated the other child-oriented activities as if those were allowed by mother. When she included the fast-food restaurant, her mother remarked in irony: "Yes, as a solution in case of catastrophe." The daughter immediately agreed and in good-girl manner admitted: "Exactly." She dropped the suggestion.

Sometimes mothers directly demanded that their daughters attend certain activities and daughters accepted the decision without resistance. In other cases daughters proposed to visit one of the attractions and immediately dropped their plan when their mothers opposed.

Dyads According to Preferred Strategies

In none of the dyads did daughters use just one of the strategies described above or did mothers initiate and react to their daughter's behavior in a single manner. However, they showed definite preferences. Thus, dyads can be described with regard to the strategies which characterize the particular meshing between mothers' and daughters' outlooks.

Dyad 1 (Child's age: 9; 7 years)

The predominant strategies of the daughter were *ingratiating* and *dominating*. This was achieved by embarrassing the mother (type 2 of dominating strategies, see above). In particular, attempts of domination consisted in the daughter's revelation of her mother's personal problems. The mother reacted unwillingly, but eventually conceded. Repeatedly she demonstrated how much she suffered. Obviously, she controlled her daughter by signals indicating that each independent action would hurt her. This way the daughter learned much about her mother's vulnerability and used her knowledge to manipulate her.

The relationship was emotionally close in a negative sense. Independence was interpreted as offense to the "close" attachment. The daughter was not able to enter into a more egalitarian exchange because she still needed her mother as a secure emotional base. Her attacks can be regarded as futile attempts of dissolving unilaterality. Mutual expectations remained undebated. Need for closeness and structural immobility left the mother's authority untouched.

In the long run, the combination of ingratiating and dominating strategies of the daughter may be a subtle way to overturn the system by driving unilaterality to the extreme. It is a way which demasks mother's demand of superiority by caricatured submission on the one hand and by turning the authority relationship upside down on the other.

Dyad 2 (Child's age: 9; 9 years)

The predominant strategies of the daughter were *striking a balance* and, less frequently, *thwarting*. The mother tried to avoid an open redefinition of the relationship by offering resources and opportunities from the very beginning of the game. Although she may have intended to acknowledge her daughter as an equal partner, she preempted the chance of jointly defining the situation and relationship by her anticipatory generosity.

The mother's inadequate reactions generated confusion because the daughter neither had a serious partner to negotiate with nor could she feel herself being taken seriously. Although mother and daughter seemed to be in good emotional connection, many misunderstandings occurred. By pretending to be her daughter's peer, the mother hid her superiority and failed to present a clear and understandable position which could have been challenged by her daughter. Confused terms of negotiation hampered the construction of meanings and relationship definitions shared by both partners.

Dyad 3 (Child's age: 10; 9 years)

The predominant strategies of the daughter were *cooperation*. The mother sensitively reacted to her daughter's demands. She did not act as a "peer" but attended to her adult perspective. Because of her mother's open position the daughter could freely express her intentions. At the same time she knew that she had to take into account her mother's wishes respectfully. The mutual interest in understanding the other generated cooperation.

Although playing the game was a test of their relationship definition, the situation was not stressful for mother and daughter. The mother obviously enjoyed her competitive daughter and appreciated her competent attempts at persuasion. The daughter tried to achieve better mutual understanding within the relationship rather than to separate herself from her mother. The mutual acceptance of being different from one another and the confident expectation that challenges can be met promoted open negotiation of roles and game decisions.

Dyad 4 (Child's age: 12; 2 years)

The predominant strategies of the daughter were *cooperating and striking a balance*. The daughter was willing to respect her mother's responsibility which made the mother reluctant to agree with electronic games and action movies. Thus, the daughter strove for compromises which the mother understood as agreement and not as an offer which deserves a counteroffer in response. The mother rigidly adhered to her rejecting attitude toward the attractions.

Thus, the daughter felt betrayed as a partner of play who has the right to pursue own goals. Therefore, she switched from cooperation to the demonstration of equality. Since she did not succeed in getting her mother's respect, she and her mother were disappointed at the end of the game. The emotional distance made the mother insensitive to her daughter's demands, which clearly differed from the rigid adult view of her mother. Thus, the dyad was unable to integrate individual perspectives flexibly.

Dyad 5 (Child's age: 9; 0 years)

The predominant strategies of the daughter were *ingratiating* and *dominating* which, in contrast to dyad 1, was achieved by commanding and harassing (type 1 of dominating strategies, see above). She either harshly pushed her goals (dominating) or pretended to be a helpless child (ingratiating). Her behaviors were extremely inconsistent, ranging between being deferential and obedient on the one side and disrespectful and tormenting on the other. The mother rarely took the initiative alone. The few times she tried to contribute, she kindly asked her daughter whether she would like to accept her suggestion.

The daughter's behaviors may be understood as a reaction to mother's passive and unclear behaviors. She seemed to seek a more reciprocal exchange between her and her mother, but achieved the opposite by her provocative behavior. The more she harassed her mother, the more her mother withdrew in order to save face.

Both mother and daughter failed to communicate clear expectations. The mother was unable to correct her daughter's inadequate behaviors, and the daughter was unable to compensate for her mother's lacking initiative. Although she looked rather self-reliant, her behaviors did not represent autonomy.

Dyad 6 (Child's age: 13; 0 years)

Predominant strategies of the daughter were *thwarting* and *striking a balance*. More than the other five mothers, this mother stressed her role as responsible authority in the game situation. All the time she educated her 13-year-old daughter as if she were still a small child.

The embarrassed daughter repeatedly tried to thwart her mother's control efforts. The mother did not react to her daughter's signals communicating that the interaction was unsatisfactory. Instead, she increased the distress until she found no other solution than terminating the game. Thus, the daughter's attempts at establishing more egalitarian cooperation were broken off.

The development of more autonomy was hampered by the mother's rigidity. But there were indications that the mother will give up her unilateral claims. As the emotional base of the relationship seemed to be safe, the transformation of the relationship can be expected as the result of continuing negotiation processes in near future.

DISCUSSION

Analyses of the interactions of mothers and daughters corroborate the notion that mothers do not require strict obedience from their daughters in case of dissent about the next steps to be planned in the game. They try to integrate their daughters' perspectives and suggestions into an agreed procedure. Perhaps they would even call their attempts negotiations by which they try to win their daughters' approval of their proposals. Closer inspection of mothers' operations demonstrates, though, that mothers use a variety of subtle strategies in order to maintain control over interactions which are still predominantly unilateral.

Apparently mothers still consider themselves responsible for acceptable behaviors in this situation. Their control intentions do not so much refer to winning the game rather as to maintaining their superior position within the relationship and with regard to educational objectives. None of the mothers, however, openly claimed that they want to impose their educational objectives or to manage the situation. Instead mothers used indirect procedures (e.g., seductive scene-setting, emotional coercion, unclarity about their real goals, exploitation of their financial position, or even tricks and deceptions) as means of pursuing their goals. Overall this was not done in an unfriendly manner, although tensions were clearly perceivable in most dyads.

The behaviors we have described show that none of the daughters from the ages of 9 to 13 years was willing to accept her mother's unilateral control in this kind of a situation. *The egalitarian play situation may have strengthened the girls' awareness of their mothers' attempts of controlling game and relationship.* However, the analyses of the interactions show that the girls were not primarily play-oriented, but were concerned about the quality of the relationship. Remarkably, no daughter chose a strategy aimed at separation. All girls were seeking a transformed relationship.

In dyad 3, which represents a successful adaptation to a new pattern of reciprocity, we could observe that the daughter was eager to explore her role as a partner in negotiations with the mother. Dyad 2 showed that the problem of redefining the relationship cannot be bypassed. Since the new quality of exchange is such an essential step in the parent–child relationship, the new role cannot be conceded as a gift, but must be explored in situations which do not conceal the real differences between an adult parent and a juvenile daughter.

The older the daughters were, the more competently they were able to express the inadequacy of their mothers' behaviors. They applied poignant procedures in order to manifest their demands for more respect and egalitarian participation. For example, the older daughters demonstrated that they could understand the mother–daughter relationship from a third-person perspective. They knew the intentions and expectations of their mothers very well and used their knowledge when they ignored or ridiculed their mothers' demands or when they reacted indulgently, although their mothers expected them to be impressed by their criticism or pressures.

These strategies often strikingly disclosed the procedures by which mothers tried to disguise their attempts of dominating the game. As they counteract mothers' objectives, daughters use strategies they cannot have learned in the mother–child interactions, although the mother–daughter interactions are an appropriate field of application for further elaboration of these strategies.

These increased competencies do not necessarily immediately generate interaction patterns which establish sincere egalitarian exchange. First and above all, the sophisticated competencies are a vehement reaction to the imbalanced relationship. It is uncertain what the result of these efforts will be in the ongoing relational development. We are not sure that all parents and children will be able to transform their relationship so that parents and children can interact as autonomous, as well as connected, persons.

The girls in the dyads seemed to be in different phases of the reformulation of the mother–daughter relationship, a change that begins in middle childhood. The girl of dyad 1 had the intention to get more leeway for deciding for herself what she wants to do. She was not ashamed when she made her mother treat her as a helpless little girl in order to receive what she wanted. In contrast, the girls of dyads 4 and 6 wanted to be autonomous in order to be emancipated from their mothers' demands on how they should behave as young adolescent girls. These girls felt ashamed about their mothers' inadequate attempts of exerting control. The demands of the girls in dyads 2 and 5 represented an intermediate stage between the unreflected conception of the girl from dyad 1 and the more developed conceptions of the girls from dyads 4 and 6. Both girls were unsatisfied with the confusing ways their mothers reacted without being able to present their own clear positions.

We do not have enough cases to construct a developmental model. The only girl who has achieved relatively respectful terms of negotiation with her mother (dyad 3) was 10 years and nine months old; the girls with relatively poor conceptions of their roles toward their mothers were still 9 years old, and the girls with more elaborated conceptions were 12 or 13 years old. The behaviors observed within dyad 4 give the impression that the best point of time at which the mother–daughter relationship could have been reshaped was missed already. Perhaps developmental processes of the separation type start from these kinds of futile attempts at renegotiating the relationship.

Although the daughters in most of our dyads were severely struggling for the transformation of the relationship, we do not conclude that these processes must be overshadowed by deep crises and serious fights. Dyad 3 is an example of an interaction in which the distinctness of perspectives and intentions was not denied but openly discussed. This dyad reminds us that we must not have too simple an idea of how a more balanced relationship can be achieved. Mother cannot become a peer, and the child cannot be raised to adult status. Perhaps a more adequate conception would state that equality in the mother–daughter relationship consists of the mutual recognition of different perspectives and responsibilities without confusing the roles. Somehow the unilaterality of the parent–child relationship will not disappear as children do not deny that the parent is more competent and more experienced than the child in many domains of life.

We presume that this kind of a relationship based on mutually recognized differences can be continued through adolescence. It is based on mutual respect between a concerned parent and a considerate preadolescent and adolescent. This relationship offers the combination of autonomy and protection which children at this age still need, although self-initiated and self-maintained peer relationships have become an important part of their lives. Presumably, this parent–child relationship requires further renegotiations in early and later adulthood.

Can mothers win? Of course, mothers can win the game, and their daughters would not object or be unsatisfied with this outcome of the game if the negotiation process of the game offered them appropriate opportunities of exchanging views, convincing each other, and jointly agreeing on procedures. When this kind of exchange did not take place in our play sessions, the game sometimes was finished before all attractions were visited (this occurred in 17 of 50 cases of the total sample). The motivation of either or both mothers and daughters was lost when mothers discovered that daughters were permanently resisting their game management or daughters found that they had no chance to influence the game in a fair way. But also when mother and daughter succeeded in finishing the game under these unilateral conditions of negotiating, mothers and daughters did not enjoy the outcome. It was not accepted, because the production of the success offended basic assumptions of how to play a game, or how to interact between mother and daughter at the age of middle or late childhood.

The observations show that both mothers and daughters can win the game when both respect each other. This definition of the game situation is an example of how to define the mother–daughter relationship in general. We assume that it is this kind of relationship which daughters are also seeking to achieve in everyday life when they are leaving childhood. Our selection included just one dyad in which the transformed type of mother–daughter relationship emerged. In the total sample, 14 mothers (28%) could be assigned to the interaction type which is represented by the mother of dyad 3. Thus, our selection of dyads demonstrates the variety of reactions to the problem and not the empirical distribution of the solutions that can be achieved by mothers and daughters already in middle and late childhood.

REFERENCES

Alsaker, F. D. (1995). Is puberty a critical period for socialization? *Journal of Adolescence, 18,* 427–444.

Bigelow, B. J., Tesson, G., & Lewko, J. H. (1996). *Learning the Rules: The Anatomy of Children's Relationships.* New York: Guilford.

Bronfenbrenner, U. (1985). Freedom and discipline across the decades. In G. Becker, H. Becker, & L. Huber (Eds.), *Ordnung und Unordnung* [Order and Disorder] (pp. 326–339). Weinheim, Germany: Beltz.

Cooper, C. R., & Carlson, C. I. (1991). *Conflict negotiation in early adolescence: Links between family and peer relational patterns.* Paper presented at the Meeting of the Society for Research in Child Development, Seattle, WA, 1991.

Dekovic, M. (1991). *The Role of Parents in the Development of Child's Peer Acceptance.* Den Haag, The Netherlands: CIP–Gegevens Koninklijke Bibliotheek.

Du Bois-Reymond, M., & Ravesloot, J. (1995). The role of parents and peers in the sexual and relational socialization of adolescents. In F. Nestmann & K. Hurrelmann (Eds.), *Social Support and Social Networks in Childhood and Adolescence* (pp. 217–239). Berlin, Germany: de Gruyter.

Duck, S. (1993). *Learning About Relationships.* Newbury Park, CA: Sage.

Fend, H. (1994). *Die Entdeckung des Selbst und die Verarbeitung der Pubertaet* [The Discovery of the Self and Coping with Puberty]. Bern, Switzerland: Huber.

Flannery, D., Montemayor, R., Eberly, M., & Torquati, J. (1993). Unraveling the ties that bind: Affective expression and perceived conflict in parent–adolescent interactions. *Journal of Social and Personal Relationships, 10,* 495–509.

Grotevant, H. D., & Carlson, C. I. (1987). Family interaction coding systems: A descriptive review. *Family Process, 26,* 49–74.

Grotevant, H. D., & Cooper, C. R. (1985). Patterns of interaction in family relationships and the development of identity exploration in adolescence. *Child Development, 56,* 415–428.

Hofer, M., & Pikowsky, B. (1993). Partnerintentionen und die Produktion von Argumenten in konfliktaeren Diskussionen [Intentions in conflictual discussions and the production of arguments]. *Zeitschrift fuer Entwicklungspsychologie und Paedagogische Psychologie, 25* (4), 281–296.

Hoppe-Graff, S., & Keller, M. (1988). Einheitlichkeit und Vielfalt in der Entwicklung des Freundschaftskonzeptes [Uniformity and diversity in the development of friendship concepts]. *Zeitschrift fuer Entwicklungspsychologie und Paedagogische Psychologie, 20* (3), 195–213.

Kobak, R. R., Cole, H. E., Ferenz-Gillies, R., & Fleming, W. S. (1993). Attachment and emotion regulation during mother–teen problem solving: A control theory analysis. *Child Development, 64,* 231–245.

Kruger, A. C., & Tomasello, M. (1986). Transactive discussions with peers and adults. *Developmental Psychology, 22,* 681–685.

Martin, P., Halverson, C., Olsen, S., Pesce-Trudell, A., & Dumka, L. (1993). Generationsunterschiede in elterlicher Erziehung [Generation differences in parental education]. *Psychologie in Erziehung und Unterricht, 40,* 43–52.

Olson, D. H., McCubbin, H. I., Barnes, H. L., Larson, A. S., Muxen, M. J., & Wilson, M. A. (1989). *Families—what makes them work.* Newbury Park, CA: Sage.

Parke, R. D., & Kellam, S. G. (Eds.). (1994). *Exploring Family Relationships with Other Social Contexts.* Hillsdale, NJ: Erlbaum.

Piaget, J. (1971). *The Language and the Thought of the Child.* New York: Hartcourt & Brace. (Original work published 1926.)

Schneewind, K. A. (1995). Familienentwicklung [Family development]. In R. Oerter & L. Montada (Eds.), *Entwicklungspsychologie* [Developmental psychology] (3rd ed., pp. 128–166). Weinheim, Germany: Psychologie Verlags Union.

Schneewind, K. A. (1996). Gesellschaftliche Veraenderungswahrnehmung und Wandel des elterlichen Erziehungsstils im Generationenvergleich [Perceptions of social change and changes of parenting styles in generational comparison]. In H. P. Buba & N. F. Schneider (Eds.), *Familie zwischen gesellschaftlicher Praegung und individuellem Design* [Families Between Societal

Influence and Individual Design] (pp. 117–128). Opladen, Germany: Westdeutscher Verlag.

Schuster, B. (1997). *Konstruktionen sozialer Wirklichkeit in Interaktionen zwischen Muettern und Kindern* [Constructions of social reality in interactions between mothers and daughters]. Unpublished doctoral dissertation, Free University of Berlin.

Selman, R. L. (1980). *The Growth of Interpersonal Understanding*. Cambridge, MA: Harvard University Press.

Simmons, R. G., & Blyth, D. A. (1987). *Moving Into Adolescence*. Hawthorne, NY: Aldine de Gruyter.

Steinberg, L., & Silverberg, S. B. (1986). The vicissitudes of autonomy in early adolescence. *Child Development, 57,* 841–851.

Sullivan, H. S. (1983). *Die interpersonale Theorie der Psychiatrie* [The Interpersonal Theory of Psychiatry]. Frankfurt, Germany: Fischer. (Original work published 1953.)

Vuchinich, S. (1987). Starting and stopping spontaneous family conflicts. *Journal of Marriage and the Family, 49,* 591–601.

Vuchinich, S., Angelelli, J., & Gatherum, A. (1996). Context and development in family problem solving with preadolescent children. *Child Development, 67,* 1276–1288.

Youniss, J. (1980). *Parents and Peers in Social Development: A Sullivan-Piaget Perspective*. Chicago: University of Chicago Press.

Youniss, J., & Smollar, J. (1985). *Adolescent Relationships with Mothers, Fathers, and Friends*. Chicago: University of Chicago Press.

Chapter 3

Experiments Using the Role-playing Method in The Study of Interactive Behavior*

Manfred Hofer
University of Mannheim

Heike Buhl
University of Jena

Research on verbal interaction between adolescents and parents has found a close association between verbal interaction and adolescent–parent relationships (Hakim-Larson & Hobart, 1987; Hofer & Pikowsky, 1993a). Modes of interaction are viewed as expressions of adolescents' struggle for autonomy in parent–child relations (Grotevant & Cooper, 1985), and are seen as a means by which that relationship develops and changes (Tesson & Youniss, 1995). This chapter presents an experimental approach to the study of adolescent development in family relations. We first introduce our theoretical model and then discuss the experimental approach in general. As experimental research regarding parent–adolescent relations is rare, we explore the question of whether this approach can actu-

* This work was supported by the German Research Foundation in the Special Research Unit 245, Speech and Situation, Heidelberg / Mannheim. Thanks are extended to Claudia Hepper, Carmen Himmeroeder-Schmidt, Christine Krettek, Thomas Lege, and Karsten Tomnitz for assistance in the studies and to Darcy Bruce Berry for her assistance in preparing the English text.

ally answer developmental questions in adolescent research. Next we describe two experiments in which participants assumed the role of a daughter in a situation where her goal conflicts with that of her mother. Findings support individuation theory and suggest that experimental methods may be useful for exploring questions about adolescent development.

A MODEL OF INTERACTIVE LANGUAGE PRODUCTION

Our model of interactive language production argues that both local and global determinants influence an individual's intentions regarding communication, and those intentions influence verbal behavior (see Figure 1). Global determinants include the individual's goals, the relationship between the interlocutors, and situational and procedural knowledge. Local determinants include aspects of the preceding utterances such as content, verbal surface, and one's perception of the illocution.

The relationship between the interlocutors is thought to be an important global determinant of their interaction (Forgas, 1985; Levelt, 1989). Individuation theory holds that in the relationship between parents and adolescents, adolescents move away from dependence on their parents and construct a *separate* self. At the same time, they seek to remain *connected* to their parents. Thus, we expect the verbal behavior of adolescents to vary based on these constructs.

In addition to relational constructs, individual parameters are also important global determinants. Discourse can be seen as a device for reaching a specific goal by means of a verbal utterance (Levelt, 1989). Thus the direction or quality of the interlocutor's goal is a major determinant of speech production (Tracy & Coupland, 1990). For instance, conflict discourse is characterized by incompatible goals (Bavelas, Black, Chovil, & Mullet, 1990), hence argumentation or compromise are expected to occur. However, both the content of a goal and its significance may influence an utterance (Gruber, 1996; Kotthoff, 1993). For example, when an adolescent strives very hard toward a goal that is incompatible with the parents' wishes, his or her verbal behavior will not be the same as it would be in the same situation where the goal is less important.

Because a dialogue is interactive in nature, local determinants also affect the production of an utterance. An individual's utterance must be logically related to the preceding utterances. To be coherent the speaker has to take into account the propositional content of the partner's utterance (Craig & Tracy, 1983) and to adapt to the verbal surface of the foregoing utterance (Halliday & Hasan, 1976). Most important, however, the speaker's reaction is determined by his or her perception of the partner's intention, the perceived illocution. For instance, if a daughter interprets a parent's question

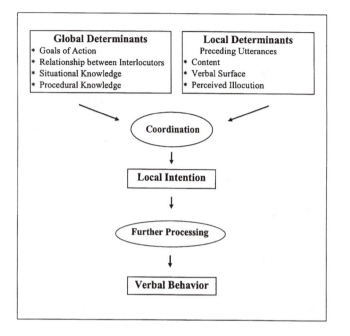

FIGURE 1.   Model of interactive language production.

as a request that she act in a specific way, she might react antagonistically, whereas she might give a quiet answer if she believes the parent is merely asking for information.

Global and local determinants are coordinated, and the resulting discourse generally displays sequential regularities. For example, in mother–daughter conflict discourse, counterarguments are often followed by counterarguments, rejections are followed by rejections, and acceptances are followed by acceptances (Hofer, Pikowsky, Fleischmann, & Spranz-Fogasy, 1993). However, sequences differ by the age and the sex of the adolescent (Vuchinich, 1987).

The preceding coordination results in a specific local intention (see Levelt, 1989), or intention to bring about or create a certain effect on the partner. This intention then leads to specific verbal behavior designed to achieve the speaker's goal.

The next step is to adopt an appropriate method for studying the causal influences of these postulated determinants. An experimental approach was selected because the independent variables can be manipulated under controlled conditions. In this situation we controlled the discourse situation by having adolescents roleplay a dialogue with the mother in each vignette.

AN EXPERIMENTAL APPROACH TO THE STUDY OF
FAMILY INTERACTION

Rationale

In adolescent and family research, properties of relationships are regularly studied using questionnaires or interviews (e.g., Steinberg & Silverberg, 1986; Youniss & Smollar, 1985). When the focus is on verbal behavior, it is standard practice to record discourse which is naturally occurring (Vuchinich, 1987) or elicited by some special task (Grotevant & Cooper, 1985). These methods have also been combined to gain insight into associations between the two sources of data (see, e.g., chapter 4, this volume). As long as studies are descriptive in nature, these methods have enormous strengths. There is no better way to assess real phenomena than to catch them in genuine and pure form in their natural context.

Such cross-sectional designs, however, are insufficient in theory-building research in which determinants of phenomena are to be identified. For example, studies which have revealed links between the perceived relationship between mother and daughter and their verbal interaction do not allow us to make causal statements. Furthermore, certain variables are confounded with the variables of theoretical interest. For example, the age of the participating adolescents is a primary confounding variable as separateness is assumed to increase during adolescence. Moreover, it is difficult to study local determinants without performing experiments. A single utterance depends on the whole foregoing dialogue and its situational context, which cannot be controlled in natural conversations. In natural conversations, one cannot isolate a special feature of a preceding utterance from others occurring simultaneously, nor can one isolate the dialogue from its specific situational context.

The disadvantages of the experimental approach lie primarily in the realm of external validity (Campbell & Stanley, 1963). As so few experimental studies have been done with regard to this realm of adolescent development, the best way to determine strengths and weaknesses is to perform experiments and discuss each experiment in terms of its contribution to theory.

In our study, female participants were asked to take the role of a daughter and were given information concerning the situation. The independent variables were varied by providing the participants in the experimental groups with different information. In this situation, participants must put themselves in a given role and act as if the situation were real. Participants know that it is an "as if " situation, and it is crucial that they succeed in taking the role (Sader, 1986). As it might be difficult for an adolescent to take the role of a daughter confronted with a mother in an experimental relationship—especially if she actually has a quite different relationship to her real mother—it is important to assure that participants view the situation as realistic and understand what it would be like to be in such a situation. Thus, one must employ a manipulation check to ensure validity of the data.

Role-playing methods have been applied successfully in several experiments investigating verbal interactions. For example, Piontkowski (1988) employed a role-playing approach to investigate language production in situations of restriction, and Grabowski-Gellert and Winterhoff-Spurk (1988) conducted a role-playing experiment to study the relationship between verbal and nonverbal messages occurring in requests under different relational conditions.

A special form of role-playing experiment requires the participants to imagine the situation described without displaying real behavior (Mixon, 1977; Sader, 1986; see also Buhl, 1996). This form of role-playing experiment allows one to present the set of instructions to the participants in writing and allows the participants to react in a written mode. In our experiments, the adolescent participants read the description of a conflict situation between mother and daughter and the discourse that followed. They were asked to write down an utterance "as they would react verbally in the role of this daughter."

As this is a special form of role-playing, the pros and cons of a written versus oral response must be considered. The obvious advantage of a written response is its economy. In our case, the investigation took place in the classroom and the utterances did not have to be transcribed. On the other hand, written responses present the problem of inferring from written to oral language production. From a theoretical point of view, even if the determinants of language production are assumed to be the same, they could be processed in different ways (Grabowski, 1996; Guenther, 1993). Empirical studies comparing oral and written utterances have led to different results depending on the communication situation, the type of discourse, and the propositional content of the utterance (Bourdin & Fayol, 1994; Hidi & Hildyard, 1983; Horowitz & Newman, 1964; Portnoy, 1973; Tannen, 1982). Because of equivocal results, the feasibility of using written instead of oral language must be examined in each case. Most of the role-playing experiments reported in this chapter were conducted using written instructions and responses. However, in order to assess the validity of these experiments, an additional role-playing experiment with oral speech production was also conducted.

DAUGHTERS' UTTERANCES IN MOTHER–DAUGHTER CONFLICT

We used role-playing experiments to investigate the model described above. The participants were native German-speaking girls between 14 and

18 years of age. They were visited in their school class where they read a text in which they were asked to put themselves in the place of a daughter. A description of the relationship between this daughter and her fictitious mother was given. The relationship described varied in the degree to which mothers and daughters expressed connectedness and separateness. Given this background information, a well-known conflict situation in which mother and daughter have incompatible goals was described (Montemayor, 1983; Oswald, 1980). The mother reminds the daughter that she is expected to spend Sunday with the family visiting "Aunt Heidrun" but the daughter would rather meet with her friends at an ice cream parlor. (See Appendix A for the English translation.)

The daughter's goal was described as either very important or not so important. To ensure that the participants understand the information provided, they were asked to describe the daughter's relationship with the mother and the goal in the conflict situation. After this, the instructions were given once more and participants read a conflict discourse between mother and daughter followed in a written manner. The discourse was presented like a comic strip. Balloons were printed on a photo of a kitchen with drawings of a mother and a daughter. The English translation of the dialogue is:

Daughter: Susi has asked me if I can go to Napoli's this afternoon. A couple of kids from our class are going to meet there.
Mother: Well, it looks as if you can't go. You know we're going to Aunt Heidrun's today. You told her you can't, I hope.
Daughter: No, not yet. Oh Mom, I'd much rather stay here and go to Napoli's with my friends than to go to Aunt Heidrun's.
Mother: But it's important to me that we spend the weekend doing things together as a family.

The local determinants were varied by changing the last utterance of the mother (proargument, counterargument, rejection). The strip indicated that after the mother's reaction the dialogue would continue. The participant was asked to write down what she spontaneously would say next. These written utterances were the basis for ascertaining the dependent variables.

Following the participants' reaction, a questionnaire was presented. The participants were asked to indicate the intention they pursued with their utterance. As a manipulation check they were asked to describe the given situation concerning relationship, goal, and the function of the mother's last utterance. Furthermore, participants were asked about the validity and authenticity of the given situation and the mother–daughter relationship. The naturalness of the relationship between mother and daughter was rated by the participants on a scale from 1 (very artificial) to 5 (very natural). The mean score was 3.53 (*SD* = 1.20). The participants also rated the success in taking the role of the daughter in the given situation on a scale from 1 (none at all) to 5 (very successful). The mean score was 3.85 (*SD* = 1.23). All participants, even those who scored low (1 or 2) indicated they knew the conflict over spending the Sunday with the family from their own experience or from descriptions by friends. There were no significant differences between conditions or between participants of different ages on these variables. Thus, the scenario chosen was accepted by the participants and they seemed to succeed in assuming the role of the daughter. Finally, the participants filled in two scales which measured "connectedness" and "separateness" to their own mother (Hofer & Pikowsky, 1993a).

Two experiments were conducted using this method. In the first, the influence of local determinants on verbal utterances was investigated, and in the second the influence of global determinants was examined.

Local Determinants of Verbal Utterances

According to the model of interactive speech production, the mother's last utterance immediately preceding the daughter's reaction should influence the daughter's statement. Analyses of sequences in quasi-natural discourse led to the expectation that a mother's simple rejection of the daughter's preceding preference would elicit more rejections by the daughter, as opposed to arguments. A counterargument and a proargument were predicted to elicit more counterarguments (Hofer, Pikowsky, Fleischmann, & Spranz-Fogasy, 1993). As the daughters' utterances should be coherent, they were expected to refer to topics present in the mother's argument.

A total of 61 adolescent girls were randomly assigned to one of three conditions: Following the last statement of the daughter, the mother: a) supported her own position with a proargument, "But it's important to me that we spend the weekend doing things together as a family," b) weakened the position of the daughter with a counterargument "You'll still be able to see your friends a lot," or c) rejected the daughter's argument "That's not possible, Julia."

The participants' utterances had a length of no more than seven units, each of which consisted of an independent statement referring to a specific topic. They were categorized according to the Mannheim Argumentation Category System (Hofer & Pikowsky, 1993b) in which units are assessed as having the discourse organizing functions of "initiatives," (requests, proposals, questions) "reactions," or arguments. Arguments refer to the position of the speaker or the partner. Possible relations to the position of the speaker are to support or to explain one's own position ("proargument") or to modify one's own argument. Possible relations to the position of the partner are to accept, to reject, or to weaken her position ("counterargument"). Furthermore, it was assessed whether a unit focused on "the speaker," "the partner," "both," "something or somebody external," or "general matters." The results reported in attained $p > .05$ and were tested using procedures for nominal scales. Trends ($p > .10$) are pointed out as such.

As expected, the participants' utterances varied depending on the mother's last statement. As a reaction to the mother's rejection, the participants uttered more questions of justification, fewer counterarguments, and as a trend fewer acceptances than in the other two conditions. Reacting to a proargument, daughters more frequently proposed alternative ways of dealing with the problem at hand. Daughters probably expected a mother speaking about her own position to be more open to their proposals. In these utterances more references are made to "both," which can be interpreted as a device of family coherence used by the mother. Hence, variation of the local determinants did influence aspects of a following utterance.

Global Determinants of Verbal Utterances

The second experiment was conducted to investigate the influence of the relational factors "connectedness" and "separateness" and the importance of the daughter's goal in the conflict situation as global determinants of verbal behavior in the model of interactive language production. Concerning the independent variable "goal significance," it was expected that participants in the condition of an important goal would try harder to reach it by using more initiatives and arguments than participants with low goal significance. Also, more counterarguments were expected to be used as a means of weakening the mother's position. Finally, it was predicted that the daughter would be less likely to modify her own position and accept the mother's position when the goal was important.

With regard to connectedness, small group research suggests that a high level of group cohesion goes along with more drive and involvement (see Evans & Dion, 1991; Stogdill, 1972), expressed in the category of initiatives. Following individuation theory, highly connected persons should express more acceptances, fewer rejections, and more references to the partner or both interlocutors than less connected participants. Participants with a high degree of separation should explain and support their own position and refer to themselves as individuals more often than participants whose separateness is less advanced. Highly separated participants should also weaken and reject the arguments of the mother more often.

The conflict situation and the goal of the participants taking the role of the daughter were the same for all participants. The three independent variables "connectedness," "separateness," and "goal significance" resulted in a 2 × 2 × 2 design. A total of 131 adolescent girls participated in the experiment, 15 to 18 per condition.

Relational parameters of connectedness and of separateness were varied by giving, the participants different descriptions of the daughter's relationship to the fictitious mother. The descriptions were as follows:

Connectedness

High: Your mother's views are very important to you.
This is partly expressed in the fact that you are willing to look at things from her side.

Low: Your mother's views are not very important to you at the moment.
This is partly expressed in the fact that you are not willing to look at things from her side.

Separateness

High: You are not afraid to stand up for your own opinions in talking to your mother.
If you don't accept something, it is easy for you to talk to her about it.

Low: You are still afraid to stand up for your own opinions in talking to your mother.
If you don't accept something, it is not easy for you to talk to her about it.

Goal significance was also presented using two levels. Half of the participants were informed that reaching the goal was very important to them and half of the participants were informed that it was not particularly important to them.

Goal significance

High: It is very important to you to reach your goal of going to the ice cream parlor! Therefore, you try to make it clear to your mother that you want very badly spend the afternoon with your friends instead of going to your aunt's. It is very important to you that you reach this goal.

Low: It is not particularly important to you that you reach your goal of going to the ice cream parlor! Therefore, you try to make it clear to your mother that you would rather spend the afternoon with your friends than go to your aunt's. However, it is not so important to you that you attain this goal.

The questions regarding the naturalness of the relationship and the success in taking the role of the daughter in the given situation were answered satisfactorily. However, we found significant interactions between separateness and goal importance. The combination of low separateness with an unimportant goal was considered to be more difficult to imagine. Interestingly, the participants' age[1] had an effect on their assessment of the induced relationship. Since separateness and age tended to interact, younger participants were better able to imagine low separateness, whereas older participants had greater success with a high degree of separateness. Possibly, role-taking is made easier when the role is similar to one's own current feeling or experience.

The frequencies of category use were analyzed by means of log-linear analyses. As no interactions were found, the results of χ^2-procedures were reported (see Table 1).

We found that goal significance explained most of the effects. Given an important goal, participants produced significantly more arguments, and as a trend they produced fewer reactions to the mother's argument. In this condition, the mother's position was weakened more often and accepted less often than in the condition of low importance. Finally, participants with a high-priority goal uttered more references to both interlocutors, mother and daughter. Participants in the high connectedness conditions tended to produce more initiatives. They explained their own position more often and made more references to themselves than participants in the low connectedness conditions. Participants in the high separation condition referred more often to "something or somebody external"; specifically, they referred more often to Aunt Heidrun, whom to the mother wanted them to visit.

TABLE 1.   **Influence of global determinants on categories of the Mannheim Argumentation Category System.**

	Independent Variables		
Category	Separateness	Connectedness	Goal significance
Discourse Organizing			
Initiatives		+[+]	
Reactions			-[+]
Arguments			+*
on speakers' own position			
Supporting			
Explaining		+*	
Modifying			-*
on the position of the partner			
Accepting			-*
Weakening			+*
Rejecting			

Note: Findings of (χ^2 analyses. + indicates positive influence, - indicates negative influ-

To summarize, verbal behavior as reflected in the categories used to analyze the utterances seems to be affected more by individual than by relational factors. Goal significance affects the frequency of use of various categories, pointing to the fact that daughters employ verbal means to strive for their goals in a given situation. In addition, the degree of connectedness and separateness between the interlocutors affects daughters' utterances to a certain extent.

The results from the previous analyses examined the first step in the model: the role of global and local determinants on participants' utterances. We now examine the next step in the model, participants' intentions.

Participants' Intentions

The point a speaker wants to make with an utterance is an important step in interactive language production. At any moment in the discourse, the local intention is assumed to be influenced by the sum of global and local determinants. At the moment in the scenario when a daughter is about to give her response, her intention may be to argue with the mother or to flatter her. In each experiment, participants were asked for their intentions with regard to their response to the mother. The stimulus was: "With your utterance, did you want to ... ?." Sixteen items describing possible intentions were offered (see Table 2). Participants rated each intention on a scale ranging from 1 (not at all) to 5 (very strongly). As the results of the two experiments were comparable, we report on data from the second experiment. Principle-components analysis (Kaiser-criterion) with varimax rotation yielded four factors, called (1) good atmosphere, (2) provocation, (3) argumentation, and (4) asking for something. Table 2 shows the factors and the items with a loading >.5, listed in descending order of loading.

Correlations were calculated for categories of actual verbal behavior and intentions as interpreted by the participants for both sets of data. First, participants seemed to use the category of acceptances as a device for creating a good atmosphere. And, participants who said they wanted to argue had actually done so. Moreover, they often argued despite being aware of the fact that argumentation may diminish good atmosphere as the use of arguments in general—especially supporting their own position—correlated negatively with the intention to produce a good atmosphere. Finally, the intention of provocation was correlated with low verbalization of acceptances and initiatives. Thus, there are connections between the actual verbal behavior of the participants and the intentions they reported.

Analyses of variance were conducted to examine the influence of "separateness," "connectedness" and "goal significance" on the intentions. Participants with high connectedness attempted to establish a good atmosphere more than those with low connectedness. They also had higher

TABLE 2.   Intentions of the participants. Results of factor analysis.

Factor	Items (English translation)
1 good atmosphere	to indicate understanding of the mother's point of view
	to create a good atmosphere
	to assert your own will (-)
	to give way
	to work towards a compromise
	to make a proposal
2 provocation	to provoke the mother
	to attack the mother's comment
	to make clear to the mother that she can't tell you what to do
	to express anger
3 argumentation	to make clear your own point of view
	to argue
	to defend yourself
4 ask for something	to ask for something
	to persuade
	to draw a comparison

scores on the intention to argue. Participants in the important goal condition tended to strive for good atmosphere less than those with an unimportant goal, and they had significantly more desire to argue.

Less separated participants tended to understand their utterances more as a provocation than highly separated participants. This is a puzzling result. Possibly participants low in separateness are aware that their task to achieve a higher degree of separateness and provocation is seen as a means to achieve this superordinate goal. Finally, there was an interaction showing that participants in the weak separateness and important goal condition tended to ask for something more often than participants in the other groups.

Thus, intentions and verbal behavior were related in a meaningful way. These findings demonstrate that participants in the experimental conditions interpreted the written utterances as speech acts directed to another person in a specific situation even if this situation was not real for them. Creating a good atmosphere, the desire to provoke the mother, arguing, or asking for something are obviously meaningful in the role of a daughter reacting to a statement by her mother. Furthermore, these intentions were influenced by the experimentally induced independent variables in a way that makes sense.

METHODOLOGICAL ISSUES

The findings presented in this study demonstrate that global and local determinants influence conflict discourse between mother and daughter in theoretically meaningful ways. While the findings are consistent in their support of the model in Figure 1, they depend on the methodology used to obtain them. As this method is not frequently used in this realm of research, we need to ascertain that the findings are valid. In our attempt to assess the validity of the studies described above, we address potential pitfalls and benefits of the experimental approach and examine the extent to which written responses provide useful data for analysis.

Potential Pitfalls

In examining the pitfalls of our experimental approach, most findings were positive. First, we demonstrated that both global and local determinants influenced utterances and intentions in a dialogue, so some degree of internal validity can be demonstrated. The fact that the direction of effects were in line with theoretical considerations following from action and developmental theories as well as from psycholinguistic and discourse analyses provides further strength for our argument. Finally, participants indicated they were quite able to take the role provided for them. Hence, the findings appear to be valid.

However one important question remains. Why did relational variables show little influence? One possibility is that participants could imagine the situational goal but could not imagine the imposed relationship to the same degree. Despite the fact that they judged the situation as natural and the role-taking as quite successful, we cannot be sure that the manipulation was strong enough to affect verbal utterances in a powerful manner.

Another possibility is that the real relationship of the participants to their own mothers may have interacted with the imposed relationship and biased their reactions in the experimental situation. To test this objection, the actual relationship was assessed with a questionnaire, but these parameters did not significantly influence the verbal behavior of the participants. This suggests that the behavior of the participants was affected by the role they were playing, and that they were able to suppress their reactions as individual participants outside the experiment.

Another possible objection is that participants confronted with a kind of relationship which is not consistent with their own could possibly get confused. To check this, separate analyses were done with those participants for whom the imposed and the real relationship were aligned. Effects were no stronger for these participants than they were for the whole group. Thus, the information gathered so far supports the assumption that in the experimental situation the imposed conditions were more salient to the participants than was their real relationship.

Assessing Benefits of Experimental Methods

An important reason for choosing the experimental design rather than a correlational approach was to avoid confounding effects and to rule out the influence of uncontrolled variables. To assess this assumed advantage, we conducted another study in which the participants were asked to imagine the given conflict and dialogue with regard to themselves and their own mother, and to act accordingly (Himmeroeder-Schmidt, 1997). Connectedness and separateness were assessed with a questionnaire, rather than manipulated, and the goal was important for all participants. This quasi-experimental study was similar to the second experiment reported above except that it was based on the scores resulting from the actual connection and separation scales, and the participants were assigned to groups of high and low "connectedness" and "separateness." Contrary to the results of the second experiment, this study only found that less separated daughters explained their position more than separated daughters. This result needs interpretation. Why did the previous experiment show influences when "in reality" no influences were found? One interpretation is that the experiments lack external validity, and their results are not generalizable. Another possibility is that the participants of the quasi-experiment did not succeed in imagining the given situation in relation with their own mother as intended by the investigators. However, it is equally possible that confounding variables which also defined the utterance were inadvertently included in the quasi-experiment. Hence, the empirical relationship may not reflect the "real" relationship because aspects of the latter might be compensated or neutralized by uncontrolled factors. Thus, this comparative study yields results which cannot be used to argue definitely for or against the validity of the experimental approach. These findings do, however, underline the advantage of controlling extraneous influences.

Mode of Response

Lastly, the validity of the experiments depends on the assumption that the written mode of understanding and producing language is equivalent to the oral mode regarding the given research question. Naturally, reading a dialogue and writing responses is not the same as verbal interaction. To compare written and oral responses, we conducted a role-playing experiment which was equivalent to the procedure described in this chapter, except that the role-playing was done orally. The "mother" was played by a female confederate, and the first turns of the dialogue were the same as those read by the participants in the written experiment. Four additional turns followed in which the role-play mother had a rough script concerning the content and the argumentative function of her utterances, and the participants were free to speak any way they liked. Two independent variables were utilized: "separateness" and "goal significance." High connectedness was induced in all experimental groups. The responses to the mother's argument, "But it's important to me that we spend the weekend doing things together as a family," were analyzed and compared with the written responses of the second experiment described above.

The contents and reasons given by the participants in both studies were highly similar. The number of words was higher in the written experiment, and the written units were more complex than the verbal units, but there were no differences in the number of information units produced in the two studies. Participants in the significant goal condition produced more arguments than participants in the insignificant goal condition. They also accepted the position of the mother less frequently and referred to their own position more often. Highly separated daughters rejected the arguments of the mother less often. This corresponds to the intention of separated daughters not to provoke the mother.

The comparison between the oral and written experiments showed no inconsistencies. Yet the oral experiment yielded fewer effects than the written one. Possibly, in face-to-face communication, nonverbal signals such as voice and bodily communication play a predominant role (Argyle, 1975). While differences between the oral and written modes of language production requires further study, the written data seems to be quite externally valid.

DISCUSSION

Based on our examination of the arguments for and against an experimental approach to the study of verbal behavior and relationships between parents and adolescents, we cannot state that such an approach is useful in all cases. The usefulness of experiments depends on the research question and the current state of the field. In every case, the pros and cons of the experimental method must be considered carefully, and the form of response must be studied thoroughly. These data do allow us to conclude, however, that the experiment is a serious alternative to correlational approaches in this realm. We were able to trace effects of imposed relationship and goal variables on utterances even in the written format.

As discussed above, the inclusion of relationship properties is a critical factor. While it is hard to know if the experimental manipulation was sufficiently effective, the alternative of assessing the actual relationship and studying its correlation with other variables, verbal or otherwise, is not without fault.

NOTE

[1] There were no differences in mean age between the conditions.

APPENDIX

Description of the conflict situation given to the participants (English translation):

You are standing in the kitchen with your mother on a Sunday morning.

At breakfast your family talked about the fact that a visit to Aunt Heidrun is planned for today. Your aunt lives about 50 km away. It has been arranged that your family (that is, your parents, your little sister, and you) will leave home at about 11:00 a.m. to be at your aunt's in time for lunch, and then spend the afternoon there.

After breakfast you received a phone call from your friend Susi and heard that she and some friends want to meet this afternoon at the Napoli ice cream parlor.

You would rather see your friends than spend the Sunday with your family.

You have promised Susi that you will call her back in five minutes to let her know if you can come.

REFERENCES

Argyle, M. (1975). *Bodily communication*. London: Methuen.

Bavelas, J. B., Black, A., Chovil, N., & Mullet, J. (1990). Truths, lies and equivocations: The effect of conflicting goals on discourse. In K. Tracy & N. Coupland (Eds.), *Multiple goals in discourse* (pp. 135–161). Clevedon: Multilingual Matters.

Bourdin, B., & Fayol, M. (1994). Is written language production more difficult than oral language production? A working memory approach. *International Journal of Psychology, 29* (5), 591–620.

Buhl, H. M. (1996). Erwerbssituation, mentale Repraesentation und sprachliche Lokalisationen - Blickpunktinformation als Bestandteil der Raumrepraesentation [Situation of acquisition, mental representation, and verbal localization. Information on perspective as part of spacial representation]. *Sprache & Kognition, 15* (4), 203–216.

Campbell, D. T., & Stanley, J. C. (1963). Experimental and quasi-experimental designs for research in teaching. In N. Gage ((Ed.), *Handbook of research in teaching* (pp. 181–246). Chicago: Rand McNally.

Craig, T., & Tracy, K. (1983). *Conversational coherence*. Beverly Hills, CA: Sage.

Evans, C. R., & Dion, K. L. (1991). Group cohesion and performance. A meta-analysis. *Small Group Research, 22* (2), 175–186.

Forgas, J. P. (1985). *Interpersonal behaviour: The psychology of social interaction.* Kensington, NSW: Pergamon.

Grabowski, J. (1996). Writing and speaking: Common grounds and differences toward a regulation theory of written language production. In M. Levy & S. Ransdell (Eds.), *The science of writing* (pp. 73–91). Hillsdale, NJ: Erlbaum.

Grabowski-Gellert, J., & Winterhoff-Spurk, P. (1988). Your smile is my command: Interaction between verbal and nonverbal components of requesting specific to situational characteristics. *Journal of Language and Social Psychology, 7,* 229–242.

Grotevant, H. D., & Cooper, C. R. (1985). Patterns of interaction in family relationships and the development of identity exploration in adolescence. *Child Development, 56,* 415-428.

Gruber, H. (1996). *Streitgespraeche—Zur Pragmatik einer Diskursform* [Arguments. On the pragmatics of a type of discourse]. Opladen: Westdeutscher Verlag.

Guenther, U. (1993). *Texte planen—Texte produzieren* [Planning texts—producing texts]. Opladen: Westdeutscher Verlag.

Hakim-Larson, J., & Hobart, C. J. (1987). Maternal regulation and adolescent autonomy: Mother–daughter resolution of story conflict. *Journal of Youth and Adolescent, 16* (2), 153-166.

Halliday, M. A. K., & Hasan, R. (1976). *Cohesion in English.* London: Longman.

Havighurst, R. J. (1972). *Developmental tasks and education.* New York: McKay.

Hidi, S. E., & Hildyard, A. (1983). The comparison of oral and written productions in two discourse types. *Discourse Processes, 6,* 91–105.

Himmeroeder-Schmidt, C. (1997). *Der Einfluß der Beziehung zwischen Gespraechspartnern auf die Sprachproduktion im Dialog* [Verbal production in dialogue depending on the relationship between participants in conversations]. Unpublished MA thesis, University of Mannheim.

Hofer, M., & Pikowsky, B. (1993a). Partnerintentionen und die Produktion von Argumenten in konfliktaeren Diskussionen [Intentions in conflictual discussions and the production of arguments]. *Zeitschrift fuer Entwicklungspsychologie und Paedagogische Psychologie, 25* (4), 281–296.

Hofer, M., & Pikowsky, B. (1993b). Validation of a category system for arguments in conflict discourse. *Argumentation, 7,* 135–148.

Hofer, M., Pikowsky, B., Fleischmann, T., & Spranz-Fogasy, T. (1993). Argumentationssequenzen in Konfliktgespraechen [Argument sequences in conflict discussions]. *Zeitschrift fuer Sozialpsychologie, 24,* 15–24.

Horowitz, M. W., & Newman, J. B. (1964). Spoken and written expression: An experimental analysis. *Journal of Abnormal and Social Psychology, 68* (6), 640–647.

Kotthoff, H. (1993). Disagreement and concession in disputes: On the context sensitivity of preference structures. *Language in Society, 22,* 193–216.

Levelt, W. J. M. (1989). *Speaking. From intention to articulation.* Cambridge, MA: Bradford.

Mixon, D. (1977). On the difference between active and nonactive role-playing methods. *American Psychologist,* 676–677.

Montemayor, R. (1983). Parents and adolescents in conflict: All families some of the time and some families all of the time. *Journal of Early Adolescence, 3,* 83–103.

Oswald, H. (1980). *Abdankung der Eltern? Eine empirische Untersuchung ueber den Einfluß von Eltern auf Gymnasiasten* [Resignation of parents? An empirical investigation on parental influence on high-track highschool students]. Weinheim: Beltz.

Piontkowski, U. (1988). *Interaktionskonflikte. Sprechen und Handeln in Beeintraechtigungsepisoden* [Conflicts in interaction. Speech and action in episodes of impairment]. Muenster: Aschendorff.

Portnoy, S. (1973). A comparison of oral and written verbal behavior. In K. Salzinger & R. S. Feldman (Eds.), *Studies in verbal behavior: An empirical approach* (pp. 99–154). New York: Pergamon.

Sader, M. (1986). *Rollenspiel als Forschungsmethode* [Role-play as a research method]. Opladen: Westdeutscher Verlag.

Searle, J. R. (1969). *Speech acts*. Cambridge: Cambridge University Press.

Spranz-Fogasy, T., Hofer, M., & Pikowsky, B. (1992). Mannheimer ArgumentationsKategorienSystem (MAKS). *Linguistische Berichte, 141,* 350–370.

Steinberg, L., & Silverberg, S. (1986). The vicissitudes of autonomy in early adolescence. *Child Development, 57,* 841–851.

Stogdill, R. M. (1972). Group productivity, drive, and cohesiveness. *Organizational Behavior and Human Performance, 8,* 26–43.

Tannen, D. (1982). Spoken and written narrative in English and Greek. In D. Tannen (Ed.), *Coherence in spoken and written discourse* (pp. 21–41). Norwood, NJ: Ablex.

Tesson, G., & Youniss, J. (1995). Micro-sociology and psychological development: A sociological interpretation of Piaget's theory. In A. M. Ambert (Ed.), *Sociological Studies of Children* (Vol. 7, pp. 101–126). Greenwich, CT: JAI.

Tracy, K., & Coupland, N. (Eds.). (1990). *Multiple goals in discourse*. Clevedon: Multilingual Matters.

Vuchinich, S. (1987). Starting and stopping spontaneous family conflicts. *Journal of Marriage and the Family, 49,* 591–601.

Youniss, J., & Smollar, J. (1985). *Adolescent relations with mothers, fathers, and friends*. Chicago: Chicago University Press.

Chapter 4

Relationship and Family Discourse in Different Situations*

Manfred Hofer
University of Mannheim

Kai Sassenberg
University of Goettingen

The research presented in this chapter has its foundation in the assumption that characteristics of the relationship with regard to individuation shape the way parents and adolescents interact. Two distinct modes of discourse using two different coding systems are examined in an attempt to demonstrate that basic tenets of individuation theory are manifest within discourse between mothers and daughters. We explore how individual perceptions of the relationship shape verbal interactions and investigate the stability of verbal behavior across different types of discourse. Findings emphasize the importance of discourse in the process of individuation and shed light on the process by which discourse may facilitate individuation.

* This work was supported by the German Research Foundation grant Ho 649/5-1 and Special Research Unit 245 "Speech production in social context" Heidelberg Mannheim. Special thanks are extended to Birgit Pikowsky, Thomas Spranz-Fogasy, and Thomas Fleischmann for their help in data collection. Send chapter correspondence, addressed to the first author, to the University of Mannheim, Department of Education, D-68131 Mannheim, Germany.

THE IMPORTANCE OF DISCOURSE

The importance of verbal interaction is increasingly recognized, particularly by social constructivists. Social constructivist theory posits that verbal interaction is crucial in the process of knowledge acquisition and the formation of relationships. Mental entities (e.g., skills, concepts, and structures) are "appropriated" via participation in sociocultural activities (e.g., Wertsch, 1985), and by actively employing cultural tools such as language (Lawrence & Valsiner, 1993; Rogoff, 1990).

Tesson and Youniss (1995) argue that individuals construct roles and, as a consequence, their relationship patterns, through everyday interactions. Parents and adolescents renegotiate their relationship via verbal interactions such as discussions and arguments. The flow of thoughts exchanged provides experiences by which each party may begin to redefine the relationship from one in which parents maintain total control to one which becomes increasingly egalitarian.

The research presented in this chapter draws on recent approaches that view discourse as a special kind of behavioral interaction. These approaches have utilized a variety of methods to examine discourse in families with adolescents (Grotevant & Carlson, 1987; Honess & Robinson, 1993). In particular, discussions of actual conflict and planning tasks have been useful in describing parent–adolescent relationships with regard to individuation (Grotevant & Cooper, 1985; Smetana, Braeges, & Yau, 1991). This chapter examines both conflict and planning discourse with two different coding systems. We developed the first system, the Mannheim Argumentation Category System (MAKS), to describe in more detail strategies parents and adolescents use when defending their standpoints during conflict. The second system was developed by Condon, Cooper, and Grotevant (1984) to analyze planning task discourse. Together, these two systems allow us to explore how individuation progresses within family relationships. They allow us to examine the patterns of interaction that occur in discussion between parents and adolescents, explore psychological aspects of individuation associated with these patterns, and investigate the stability of discourse patterns over different types of relationships and different types of discourse.

DEVELOPMENT OF THE MANNHEIM ARGUMENTATION CATEGORY SYSTEM

Achievement of autonomous relations with parents is a central task of adolescent social development, so we developed the Mannheim Argumentation Category System (Hofer, Pikowsky, Spranz-Fogasy, & Fleischmann, 1990) to measure constructs important in this process. MAKS categorizes discourse as indicating an *initiative, a response to an initiative, an argument*, or *a reaction to an argument* (see Table 1). We propose that these aspects of argumentation facilitate adolescent individuation (e.g., Tesson & Youniss, 1995), and that examination of argumentation patterns will provide a new perspective from which to view adolescent individuation.

As individuation occurs within the context of the parent–adolescent relationship, this system incorporates ideas related to how both parents and adolescents might be expected to act based on theory. For instance, in conflictual discourse, parents tend to exert control over their adolescent while trying to maintain a good relationship. Thus, they are expected to steer the discourse and gain formal control over its flow by using initiatives such as requests, proposals, questions, acceptances, and rejections (Kruger & Tomasello, 1986). In turn, adolescents can accept, refuse, ignore, or take the lead and create response pressure for their parents.

Parents are also expected to exert cognitive control over their children by presenting information in support of their opinion (e.g., argumentative functions). Adolescents may reject parents' arguments and criticize them. They might give counterarguments in response to parents' supportive arguments, or they may maintain their own opinion. Examples of each category are found in Table 1.

From the adolescents' perspective, autonomy development entails striving for separateness from, as well as maintaining connectedness to, parents (Grotevant & Cooper, 1985; Smollar & Youniss, 1989; Steinberg & Silverberg, 1986; Youniss, 1989). Consequently, argumentation categories were developed to illuminate both processes. The construct of separateness is comprised of *independency, deidealizing parents*, and *individuation*. Independence describes the absence of childish dependency on parents, and it is evidenced by parent–child conflict which increases between early and middle adolescence (Laursen, 1995; Montemayor, 1983). Rejection of parents' initiatives is one way adolescents can exert their independence. Deidealizing describes the relinquishing of childish perceptions of parental omnipotence, and may be made manifest when adolescents doubt parents' arguments in a conflict. Individuation describes the attainment of one's own standpoint; when adolescents conceptualize themselves as separate and distinct persons. Individuation may be evidenced in a conflict when adolescents explain their position by producing reasons by way of pro-arguments, additional arguments, modifying arguments, and counterarguments (see Table 1). Simultaneously, adolescents are seen as maintaining connection with their parents. They respect them, appreciate them as persons, and feel obliged to them (Youniss & Smollar, 1985). In conflict discourse, adolescents are expected to cooperate with their parents and accept initiatives and arguments to a certain extent even when they disagree (see Table 1).

TABLE 1. Argumentation Category System: Definitions and Examples

Category	Definitions	Examples	Cohen's k
Initiative	A statement in which the speaker obviously tries to influence the behavior or the thoughts of the hearer.		.88
Request		<clean up the kitchen>	
Proposal		<you can use the other bathroom>	
Question of clarification		<what do you think about it>	
Question of justification		<why isn't that enough money>	
Response to initiative	The speaker accepts or rejects an initiative of the partner.		.90
Acceptance		<yes, I will do it>	
Rejection		<no>	
Reaction to an argument	An utterance which shows acceptance or rejection of a partner's argument without containing an argument itself.		
Acceptance of argument		D: <yes, you are right>	.94
Rejection of argument		D: <no this is not true>	.85
Argument			
Proargument	An utterance that extends an argument to justify one's position.	<I want to go out tonight> <because there is no school tomorrow>	.82
Additional argument	An utterance that adds an argument to another proargument in the same turn.	<Hans doesn't help either> <he just plays with the computer>	.81
Modifying argument	An utterance that limits or qualifies one's own statement.	<I understand that you are worrying> <but I am old enough>	.84
Counter argument	An utterance which is intended to weaken the position of the partner, e.g., which is incompatible with the position or argument of the partner.	M: <you've only known this boy for three weeks> D: <actually I've known him for six weeks>	.73

SAMPLE AND PROCEDURE

MAKS and Condon et al.'s (1984) system for coding a planning task were used to examine adolescents' individuation processes in actual discourse with their parents. This research examines discourse between mother–daughter dyads for methodological reasons. First, in triads difficulties may arise in identifying to whom an utterance is directed. For instance, a speaker can direct his or her suggestion to all present, or an utterance can be a reaction to something a third person said several turns before. When using dyads, the roles of the partners involved in the relationship are easily identifiable. For example, when Inge discusses her curfew with her mother, it is clear that Inge is speaking only to her mother. Moreover, as various main effects regarding sex of the participants and interactions between them may occur, we hold constant variance-producing variables and restrict the study to one dyadic relationship.

Sixty-one mother–daughter dyads were recruited from an industrialized German city by obtaining a random sample from the local authorities. To be included in the study, a daughter had to be between 11 and 17 years old, not earn her own money, and live with her mother in the same household. The majority of the mothers (69%) reported a middle-class background on a single-item rating; however, 11 percent reported an upper middle-class background, and 19 percent reported they were from the working class. Education of daughters was higher than mothers, which is consistent with the remainder of the population. About 42 percent attended the highest track of the German school system, 42 percent attended the middle track, and 16 percent attended the lower track (for more details see Hofer & Pikowsky, 1993b).

The participants were visited in their homes and asked to discuss a conflict which was currently relevant to them and to plan a two-week family vacation without financial limits (Hofer, 1996). The investigator audiotaped the discussions, which were later transcribed (Gutfleisch-Rieck, Klein, Speck, & Spranz-Fogasy, 1989). Immediately after the two discussions, the participants rated the discussions on several scales to assess whether the conflict had been treated in a usual way.

Two examples of transcribed discourse follow:

Example 1:   Daughter: Often I read until ten o'clock.
             Mother: That's not true.
             Daughter: Sure, you just don't know it.
             Mother: I do know when you turn off the light.

Example 2:   Mother: It should be more often.
             Daughter: Okay I do learn when I have to, but...

Mother: Yes, but not enough not enough. That's
the problem. You would get better grades.
You should work harder. That's difficult for
you but you want to finish high school by all
means and you have to invest more but you
are not ready for this.

MEASURES

Coding Discourse

In the first step of coding for MAKS, units consisting of sentences were
identified by trained raters. Next, every unit was coded according to the
system described above. To estimate reliability, 10 discourse sequences
were coded by two independent raters. Coder-correspondence was 88%
for identifying units. Interrater-reliability for the coding of the single
categories attained Cohen's kappas (Cohen, 1968) between 0.73 and
0.94 (see Table 1; for more details see Hofer & Pikowsky, 1993b). There
was no significant effect of daughters' educational level on communication. As discussions differed in length, a relative frequency score was
computed for each person by dividing the absolute frequency in each
category by the number of units produced by the person in the discussion.

Planning task discourse was recorded, transcribed, and coded according
to the manual by Condon et al. (1984). Discourse was first separated into
units which generally were a sentence. One turn could consist of several
units. Each unit was coded using this system which included the mutually
exclusive "move" dimension containing initiative categories and "reaction"
dimensions. In addition, a third dimension which consisted of "mindreads"
and "relevant comments" was coded. Table 2 provides examples of each
category. Interrater reliability for single categories attained Cohen's kappas
between .50 and 1.00.

Subjective Interpretation of Discourse

Participants were asked to indicate the degree to which items expressed the
arguments they tried to make during the discussion on a five-point scale.
Items measured control (8 items, Cronbach's alpha .85) and separation (5
items, Cronbach's alpha .69) for mothers and separation (8 items, Cronbach's alpha .77) and connection (6 items, Cronbach's alpha .80) for daughters. Items were assigned to scales by factor analysis and summed up for
each participant.

TABLE 2. Coding system of Condon, Cooper, & Grotevant (1984): Definitions, examples, reliability, and assignment to intentions and coding dimensions.

Intentions and Categories	Coding Dimension	Examples	Cohen's k
Self assertion			
Direct suggestion	move	\<I'd like to go to Italy\>	0.53
Permeability			
Acknowledgment	response	\<you might say where you want to go\>	0.66
Request for information	move	\<how far is it from Rome to Athens\>	0.94
Agreement	response	\<that's a good idea\>	0.76
Relevant comment	other	\<in Algeria there's a lot of political unrest\>	0.80
Compliance with request for action	response	\<I'll write that down right now\>	0.77
Mutuality			
Indirect suggestion	move	\<let's go to Canada\>	0.86
Initiation of compromise	response	\<we can first go to Athens and we'll fly to Miami\>	0.50
Statement of others feelings	other	\<I'm sure you want to visit the art gallery\>	0.82
Answer to request for information	response	\<that's not far away\>	0.72
Separateness			
Request for action	move	\<write that down there\>	0.70
Direct disagreement	response	\<I don't want to go to Vienna\>	0.74
Indirect disagreement	response	\<that won't be fun\>	0.60
Irrelevant comment	move	\<you know, we're missing my favorite show\>	1.00

MAKS: AN EXAMINATION OF FACE VALIDITY

Examination of conflict discourse using MAKS indicated that mothers expressed significantly more initiatives in terms of requests, proposals, and questions, and more additional and modifying arguments than daughters. Daughters produced more counterarguments, reactions to initiatives, and arguments than mothers (see Table 3). These findings support the face validity of the measure as they are consistent with what we would expect based on the theoretical underpinnings of the coding scheme. Mothers tried to exert influence over daughters by arguing their point and by retaining control over the flow of the discourse. Daughters rejected mothers' requests and proposals in order to gain independence. They questioned their mothers' position and their arguments which indicates deidealization. They argued in favor of their position to demonstrate independence. As these results are precisely what we would expect based on theory, they provide support for the face validity of this measure.

TABLE 3.   Mean percentage of mother and daughter for categories of planning and conflict discourse (matched t-test)

	Daughter	Mother	t(60)	p(t)
Planning discourse				
Irrelevant comment	,03	,45	2,47	*
Suggest action or location directly	4,47	4,24	,39	
Suggest action or location indirectly	16,23	14,16	1,46	
Request info validation	10,12	17,81	-4,02	***
Request action	1,98	4,70	-2,92	**
Initiate compromise	1,48	1,26	,69	
Agree/accept	12,76	7,94	4,36	***
Disagree directly	4,49	2,96	2,76	**
Disagree indirectly	6,21	5,63	,77	
Answer request for info/validation	12,89	4,90	4,66	***
Answer request for action	,96	,18	3,54	**
Acknowledgment	12,55	15,79	-2,62	*
Relevant comment	14,01	20,30	-4,29	***
Mindread	2,46	4,18	-4,14	***
Conflict discourse				
Request / proposal	4,76	7,40	-2,25	*
Question of clarification or justification	7,25	11,15	-2,63	*
Acceptance of initiative	4,03	1,16	4,40	***
Rejection of initiative	1,02	,60	1,63	
Acceptance of argument	11,25	7,14	3,78	***
Rejection of argument	4,89	3,04	2,85	**
Proargument	3,16	4,44	-2,21	*
Additional argument	26,36	33,01	-3,37	**
Modifying argument	4,49	6,52	-2,25	*
Counter argument	27,74	20,39	5,37	***

DISCOURSE BEHAVIOR AND RELATIONSHIP QUALITY

While these findings are compelling, previous research provides support for MAKS' discriminant validity. Pikowsky (1993) argued that, since it is widely known that people try to adapt their way of speaking to fit the partner (e.g., Herrmann & Grabowski, 1994; Snow, 1972) the type or quality of relationship adolescents have with a partner may influence the way they interact. Pikowsky (1993) used MAKS to analyze the discourse of a sample of adolescent girls discussing real conflicts in dyads with their mother, same-sex best friend, and younger sister. Results showed striking differences in discussion patterns between the three types of dyads. Mothers led the discourse and introduced moral standards while daughters played a complementary role. They reacted to mothers' actions, but the interaction tended to be oppositional. In discourse with their younger sisters, the pattern reversed. Daughters took the lead over the course and content of the discussion, and they expressed moral standards, thus forcing the sister in the complementary role. In discourse with their best friend, however, the pattern of discourse was nearly symmetrical. Pikowsky's findings suggest that the role one plays in discourse is related to the balance of power in the relationship. In situations of low power (e.g., mother–daughter relationship), daughters played a complementary role, while in situations where the balance of power is more equal (e.g., friendship) daughters' discourse took a more egalitarian style.

As these different relationships imply a different balance of power, we hypothesize that psychological processes mediate between a person's role within the relationship and differences in discourse style. We examined participants' subjective interpretations of the discourse in conjunction with the discourse data to test this hypothesis (Hofer & Pikowsky, 1993a). A significant correlation was found between daughters' understanding of their behavior as expressing separation, and their perception of separation within the relationship. Daughters who interpreted their verbal behavior as striving toward separation were less likely to accept mothers' arguments ($r = -.31; p < .01$) and more likely to produce counterarguments ($r = .25; p < .05$). Further, mothers were more likely to reject their arguments($r = .27; p < .05$). Hence, striving for separation goes hand-in-hand with argumentative and controversial verbal behavior.

THE CROSS-SITUATIONAL STABILITY OF DISCOURSE BEHAVIOR

So far the focus has been on discourse data but, in everyday family discussions, a wide range of themes are explored (e.g., curfew, time spent studying, personal problems, hopes and dreams for the future) and the character of discourse varies (e.g., businesslike, intimate, comical). While the context of the discourse may vary, the role each person plays in the relationship (e.g., mother/ daughter) is constant over all types of interactions. We now examine conflict and planning discourse to investigate how type of discourse and one's role in the relationship may influence the patterns of interaction. In doing so we investigate stability of discourse patterns and stability of asymmetry in use of initiatives, reactions, agreements, and disagreements in two types of discourse.

Research indicates that adolescents and parents discriminate between three types of interactions: normative rightness, objective facts and efficiency, and subjective authenticity (de Wuffel, 1986). Normative rightness deals with issues of family rules and regulations such as curfew, obeying parents, duties, and quarreling. Objective facts and efficiency pertains to issues such as housekeeping, homework, and school. Subjective authenticity pertains to problems, closeness, and free time.

As partners may have divergent goals in these various types of discourse, they may use different methods to achieve them. Consequently, verbal behavior might vary by type of discourse. However, as one's role within the dyad remains constant throughout all interactions, we expect some degree of similarity between types of discourse because of role effects.

We used conflict and planning discourse from 61 of the mother–daughter dyads described earlier to examine these hypotheses and questions. Conflict discourse refers to the world of normative rightness. In conflict, goals of the participants are contrary by definition. Adolescents' wish for separation and parents' wish for control may be salient as each partner wants their position to be respected. Consequently, the interaction entails negotiation, and there may be a negative emotional undercurrent.

Planning discourse, on the other hand, refers to the world of objective facts and efficiency. Parents' and adolescents' goals probably are not opposite. Partners are willing to cooperate and the exchange should facilitate properties of mutuality and symmetrical interactions.

Discourse was coded using MAKS and the Condon et al. (1984) scheme to capture specific aspects of discourse behavior related to the different tasks. Results show the role-related mother–daughter pattern as highly stable across discourse types (see Table 3). In both tasks, mothers produced more requests than their daughters, and they dominated in reinforcing their daughters with acknowledgments. Daughters, on the other hand, were much higher in response categories, thus complementing mothers' moves. They were more likely to accept mothers' moves than vice versa (e.g., answering their requests), but they also were higher in direct disagreements. Thus, mothers gave structure to the interaction while daughters responded to, or complemented, their moves. The same asymmetric behavior showed up in the content categories. Mothers made more relevant comments and changed their perspectives more often than daughters. In terms of individuation theory, both types of discourse displayed elements of early parent–child interactions and elements of adolescent dominance (Youniss, 1980).

Correlations between the scores of categories for both systems were computed to determine stability of verbal behavior in different types of discourse more closely. Because basic categories of each system did not correspond to each other, the basic categories were collapsed to equivalent higher order categories: *initiatives, reactions, agreements* and *disagreements*. Substantial correlations were found for daughters on these categories ($r = .37$ to $.50$; $p_{max} < .01$). In addition, daughters with high agreement in one type of discourse scored high in reactions and low in disagreement in the other ($|r| = .28$ to $.47$; $p_{max} < .05$). Thus, in mother–daughter discussions, daughters' behavior was relatively stable, regardless of discourse type. Mothers showed a different pattern, however. The only categories that significantly corresponded between both tasks were initiatives and disagreements ($r = .43$ and $r = .34$ respectively; $p < .01$). The correlation for reactions was only marginally significant ($r = .21$; $p < .06$), and agreement in the two types of discourse was unrelated. Hence, mothers consistently controlled the discourse, although they employed agreements, as signs of an individuated relationship, depending on the behavior of their daughters.

Finally, to capture cross-situational stability in discourse *balance* (Gottman, 1986; Watzlawick, Beavin, & Jackson, 1969), mothers' relative frequency scores were subtracted from daughters' relative frequency scores for each category. This measure displays asymmetries in utterances between mother and daughter. A score near zero means that both partners produced nearly the same amount of utterances in the respective category. Positive scores indicate daughters' predominance in the respective category while negative scores indicate mothers' predominance.

The categories in the planning task correlated positively with the respective categories in the conflict task (see Table 4). Hence, when daughters dominated reactions, initiatives, agreements, and disagreements during the planning task, they dominated in the same categories during the conflict discourse. Further, when daughters dominated agreement during either discourse, they also tended to dominate reactions while mothers tended to dominate initiatives during the other discourse. Finally, when daughters dominated in initiatives during the planning task, mothers tended to dominate in reactions during the conflict discourse.

This pattern of results suggests that speech behavior varies more by role (mother vs. daughter) than it varies by type of discourse within the same role, especially for daughters. Mothers, however, change their behavior somewhat from task to task. This difference could be caused by daughters'

TABLE 4.   Correlations of difference scores of higher order categories
(mothers' relative frequencies subtracted from daughters' relative frequencies)
between interaction tasks.

	Planning: Reactive	Planning: Initiative	Planning: Agreement	Planning: Disagreement
Conflict: Reactive	**.32	**-.35	**.38	.01
Conflict: Initiative	-,14	***.42	*-.30	.05
Conflict: Agreement	*.22	**-.33	**.34	-.10
Conflict: Disagreement	.14	-.14	.07	*.22

separation intention, which results in different reactions from mothers depending on the task.

CONCLUSION

The findings presented in this chapter provide evidence for the validity of
MAKS and suggest that examination of discourse data can shed light on the
role of verbal interactions in the development of autonomy. Specifically,
they support the idea that verbal interactions are vital in the process by
which adolescents and parents renegotiate their relationship, and they shed
light on the processes by which verbal interactions facilitate individuation
from both the adolescents' and parents' perspective.

During adolescence, youth begin striving for a perception of a self independent of parents and begin questioning parental control. As long as adolescents only refute their parents' initiatives, they take the complementary
role of the early parent–child relationship. These interactions do not provide any new experience for the interactors, because children may refuse
mothers' wishes at an early age (Kuczynski & Kochanska, 1990). However,
when adolescents rebut by introducing new information, new reasons, and
new moral standards, they may learn that they can face their parents at an
equal level and they may jointly experience a new quality of relationship. Especially in conflict discourse, adolescents in our sample surpassed mothers
in rejecting arguments and producing counterarguments, and they produced as many proarguments as their mothers. In these interactions, adolescents may learn that knowledge can be used efficiently to justify one's
standpoint and to resist mothers' attempts to control.

From an interactional standpoint, parents contribute equally to the relationship. Parents' remain active in the relationship on three levels (see Collins, 1990; Smetana, 1989). They maintain the role of educator and expect their children to comply with certain requests (compliance), they try to maintain a positive relationship (communicativeness), and they continue to transfer responsibilities to their growing children (task independence). When previously compliant adolescents begin questioning parental requests as a consequence of their separation efforts, as we saw in this chapter, parents may experience discrepancies between their expectations and the adolescents' behavior. They may first interpret the adolescents' behavior as resistance or insolence. They may learn that their arguments are no longer compelling to their child, and that they have to take into account the adolescents' point of view (Collins, 1990).

Findings indicate, however, that some adolescents are more likely than others to alter the complementary relationship style. Those who perceive themselves as striving for independence produced more counterarguments, which indicates a shift in relationship quality. Hence, individuals' perception and interpretation of their behavior provide valuable insight into the connection between verbal behavior and the quality of the relationship (Powers, Welsh, & Wright, 1994).

Finally, findings demonstrate that the transformation of the relationship can proceed at a different pace depending on the type of communication. In conflict, where the goals of each party are divergent, transformation of the relationship is more apparent. The pattern of findings regarding stability of discourse behavior suggests, however, that speech behavior varies more by role (mother vs. daughter) than it varies by type of discourse within the same role. Mothers tend to control the flow of discourse while daughters respond. While mothers retain their role in regulating the discourse even when symmetry is more pronounced (e.g., the exchange of information, ideas, and arguments), findings indicate that role dependency is even more salient for daughters. This difference may be caused by daughters' attempt to separate, which causes different reactions from mothers depending on the task.

REFERENCES

Cohen, J. (1968). Weighted kappa: Nominal scale agreement wit provision for scale disagreement or partial credit. *Psychological Bulletin, 70,* 213–220.

Collins, W. A. (1990). Parent–child relationships in the transition to adolescence: Continuity and change in interaction, affect, and cognition. In R. Montemayor, G. Adams, & T. Gullotta (Eds.), *From Childhood to Adolescence: A Transitional Period? Advances in Adolescent Development* (Vol. 2). Beverly Hills, CA: Sage.

Condon, S. L., Cooper, C. R., & Grotevant, H. D. (1984). Manual for the analysis of family discourse. *Psychological Documents, 14,* 2616.

Gottman, J. M. (1986). The observation of social process. In J. M. Gottman & J. G. Parker (Eds.), *Conversations of Friends: Speculations of Affective Development* (pp. 51–100). Cambridge, England: Cambridge University Press.

Grotevant, H. D., & Carlson, C. I. (1987). Family interaction coding systems: A descriptive review. *Family Process, 26,* 50–72.

Grotevant, H. D., & Cooper, C. R. (1985). Patterns of interaction in family relationships and the development of identity exploration in adolescence. *Child Development, 56,* 415–428.

Gutfleisch-Rieck, I., Klein, W., Speck, A., & Spranz-Fogasy, T. (1989). Transkriptionsvereinbarungen fuer den Sonderforschungsbereich 245: Sprechen und Sprachverstehen im sozialen Kontext [Transcription rules for the special research unit 245: Language production and understanding in social contexts.

Bericht Nr. 14 aus dem Sonderforschungsbereich 245: Sprechen und Sprachverstehen im sozialen Kontext [Research report No. 14 of the special research unit 245]. Universities of Heidelberg and Mannheim.

Herrmann, T., & Grabowski, J. (1994). *Sprechen: Psychologie der Sprachproduktion* [Speaking: Psychology of Language Production]. Heidelberg, Germany: Spektrum.

Hofer, M. (1996). Symmetrien und Asymmetrien in Planungsgespraechen von Mutter–Tochter Dyaden [Symmetries and asymmetries in planning discourse of mother daughter dyads]. *Zeitschrift fuer Paedagogische Psychologie, 10,* 49–60.

Hofer, M., & Pikowsky, B. (1993a). Partnerintentionen und die Produktion von Argumenten in konfliktaeren Diskussionen [Partner related intentions and the production of arguments in conflict discourse]. *Zeitschrift fuer Entwicklungspsychologie und Paedagogische Psychologie, 25,* 281–296.

Hofer, M., & Pikowsky, B. (1993b). Validation of a category system for arguments in conflict discourse. *Argumentation, 7,* 135–148.

Hofer, M., Pikowsky, B., Spranz-Fogasy, T., & Fleischmann, T. (1990). *Mannheimer ArgumentationsKategorienSystem (MAKS)* [Mannheim argumentation category system]. Bericht Nr. 22 aus dem Sonderforschungsbereich 245: Sprechen und Sprachverstehen im sozialen Kontext. Universities of Heidelberg and Mannheim.

Honess, T., & Robinson, M. (1993). Assessing parent–adolescent relationships: A review of current research issues and methods. In S. Jackson & H. Rodriguez-Tomé (Eds.), *Adolescence and its social worlds* (pp. 47–66). Hillsdale, NJ: Erlbaum.

Kruger, A. C., & Tomasello, M. (1986). Transactive discussion with peers and adults. *Developmental Psychology, 22,* 681–685.

Kuczynski, L., & Kochanska, G. (1990). Development of children's noncompliance strategies from toddlerhood to age 5. *Developmental Psychology, 26,* 398–408.

Laursen, B. (1995). Conflict and social interaction in adolescent relationships. *Journal of Research on Adolescence, 5,* 55–70.

Lawrence, J. A., & Valsiner, J. (1993). Conceptual roots of internalization: From transmission to transformation. *Human Development, 36,* 150–167.

Montemayor, R. (1983). Parents and adolescents in conflict: All families some of the time and some families most of the time. *Journal of Early Adolescence, 3*, 83–103.

Pikowsky, B. (1993). *Partnerbezogenes Argumentieren: Jugendliche Maedchen im Konfliktgespraech mit Freundin, Mutter und Schwester* [Partner Related Argumentation: Adolescent Girls' Discussions with Best Friend, Mother, and Sister]. Frankfurt, Germany: Lang.

Powers, S. I., Welsh, D. P., & Wright, V. (1994). Adolescents' affective experience of family behaviors: The role of subjective understanding. *Journal of Research on Adolescence, 4*, 585–600.

Rogoff, B. (1990). *Apprenticeship in Thinking: Cognitive Development in Social Context.* New York: Oxford University Press.

Smetana, J. G. (1989). Adolescents' and parents' reasoning about actual family conflict. *Child Development, 60*, 1052–1067.

Smetana, J. G., Braeges, J. L., & Yau, J. (1991). Doing what you say and saying what you do. Reasoning about adolescent–parent conflict in interviews and interactions. *Journal of Adolescent Research, 6*, 276–295.

Smollar, J., & Youniss, J. (1989). Transformations in adolescents' perceptions of parents. *International Journal of Behavior Development, 12*, 71–84.

Snow, C. (1972). Mothers' speech to children learning language. *Child Development, 43*, 549–565.

Steinberg, L. D., & Silverberg, S. B. (1986). The vicissitudes of autonomy in early adolescence. *Child Development, 57*, 841–851.

Tesson, G., & Youniss, J. (1995). Micro-sociology and psychological development: A sociological interpretation of Piaget's theory. In A. M. Ambert (Ed.), *Sociological Studies of Children* (Vol. 7, pp. 101–126). Greenwich, CT: JAI.

Watzlawick, P., Beavin, J. H., & Jackson, D. D. (1969). *Menschliche Kommunikation* [Pragmatics of Human Communication]. Bern, Germany: Huber.

Wertsch, J. V. (1985). *Vygotsky and the social formation of mind.* Cambridge, MA: Harvard University Press.

de Wuffel, F. J. (1986). *Attachment beyond childhood: Individual and developmental differences in parent-adolescent attachment relationships.* Unpublished doctoral dissertation, University of Nijmegen, The Netherlands.

Youniss, J. (1980). *Parents and Peers in Social Development.* Chicago: University Press

Youniss, J. (1989). Parent–adolescent relationships. In W. Damon (Ed.), *Child Development Today and Tomorrow* (pp. 379–392). San Francisco: Jossey-Bass.

Youniss, J., & Smollar, J. (1985). *Adolescent Relations with Mothers, Fathers, and Friends.* Chicago: The University of Chicago Press.

Chapter 5

Continuity and Change in Family Interactions Across Adolescence*

Peter Noack
University of Jena

Baerbel Kracke
University of Mannheim

As part of the social transitions (Steinberg, 1993) on the way to adulthood, adolescents' role in the family and their relationships with their parents must be redefined. Becoming an adult requires an increase of self-reliance and autonomy, which conflict with childhood dependencies. It is assumed that communication in the family changes its character as part of this process, and at the same time it serves to foster the transformation of family relationships (Pikowsky & Hofer, 1992). While verbal interactions in a family with an adolescent deserve particular interest on the part of developmentalists, the number of studies devoted to the micro-analysis of adolescents' family relationships is limited. Most of what we know so far is based on self-reports, which are confined to the adolescent perspective.

In the present chapter, we introduce research which follows a molecular approach examining the verbal behavior of adolescents and their parents in

* This research was funded by the German Research Council (No 213/1-1,2; Ho 649/8-1 to 4). We thank Michael Fingerle for assistance in running the Early Adolescence Study. Our thanks are extended to Andrea Moser for her involvement in the analyses of the Late Adolescence data.

the course of triadic family conversations. Longitudinal observational assessments, which were collected when adolescents were between about 12 and 18 years, provide insights into the development of family interactions during this considerable period of the adolescent transition. In this chapter, our primary objective is descriptive in nature. We want to examine patterns of continuity and change in interactional behavior across time. Drawing on individuation theory (Grotevant & Cooper, 1985; Youniss & Smollar, 1985), we expect to observe an increase in the intensity in negotiations during mid-adolescence. Moreover, a considerable transformation of family communication can be assumed to be accomplished by the time adolescents approach the age of majority when patterns of interaction should reflect a more egalitarian role system.

Our report is based on two studies. In the first one, adolescents were contacted in seventh grade and followed for two years up to the age of 15 (Noack, 1990; Noack, 1991). The second data set is from an ongoing longitudinal study (Hofer & Noack, 1992; Hofer, Noack, & Klein-Allermann, 1994; Hofer, Noack, Wild, & Kracke, 1996) which was started when adolescents were 15 years old. Data up to the age of 17 are currently available for analyses. Despite considerable similarities, such as the triadic nature of the observed family situations, the use of plan-something-together tasks (Grotevant & Cooper, 1985) to elicit interactions, and the one-year time intervals between data collections, the studies have been devised and conducted independently of each other. As such, methodological differences do not allow researchers to simply treat them as a quasi-longitudinal study of five years. The sample of the first study, for example, is confined to students attending the highest track of West German schools, whereas adolescents in the second sample are middle-track students from East and West Germany. Moreover, different instruments were employed to code the observational data. From our point of view, however, combining the information from the two studies into one chapter will provide instructive insights.

The empirical part of this chapter is organized into two sections in which we separately report on the Early and the Late Adolescent Studies. Before turning to our own research, we first discuss theoretical considerations of relationship development during adolescence and findings from earlier empirical work. Given the focus of the present chapter, a separate section is devoted to micro-analytic studies of family interactions. In the concluding discussion, we will try to draw together the empirical results of our two investigations and consider possible implications for individuation theory. A central question to be addressed will be the typical age interval which should be assumed to provide the stage for the transformation of family relationships. Our findings suggest that the process of relationship individuation may continue well into young adulthood.

CHANGES OF FAMILY RELATIONSHIPS DURING ADOLESCENCE

During the last decade, family studies and youth research have made considerable progress resulting in an increasingly differentiated portrayal of the family at adolescence (Hofer, Klein-Allermann, & Noack, 1992; Nave-Herz & Markefka, 1989; Steinberg, 1990). The variety of theoretical models and empirical approaches employed in the different studies make it difficult, however, to arrive at a comprehensive understanding. Still, there is growing agreement that earlier conceptualizations characterizing family relations during adolescence in terms of storm and stress must be abandoned due to a lack of convincing empirical support (Hill, 1987; Steinberg, 1993; cf. Collins & Laursen, 1992). At the same time, developmentalists have not adopted the reverse view stating that relationships between adolescents and their parents are characterized by pure harmony or remain unchanged in the course of the transition from childhood to adulthood.

Recent formulations of individuation theory (Grotevant & Cooper, 1985; Youniss & Smollar, 1985) set out to integrate the empirical findings and to provide a coherent account of relationship development during adolescence. Suggesting connectedness and individuality in the family as pivotal constructs, a transformation of role relations and family members' mutual perceptions is postulated to take place on the basis of sound socio-emotional bonds between adolescents and their parents. The direction of change is toward reciprocity and equality. According to this understanding, the motor of transformation is parent–adolescent communication. Explicit and implicit negotiations of adolescents' thrust toward autonomy and parental attempts to stay in control propel the process. Given the delicate balance that must be kept in the course of family individuation, it is a difficult task for both generations in the family. Nevertheless, the majority of families seem to be sufficiently successful in their efforts.

Cross-sectional studies employing instruments directly based on individuation theory (e.g., Hunter, 1984; Wilder, 1995), provided evidence for the postulated increase of mutuality among family members in the course of adolescence. Perceived parental authority does not, however, seem to fade in a linear way. Rather, the data suggest a peak shortly before or around mid-adolescence followed by a systematic decline. Likewise, Furman and Buhrmester (1992) observed an inverted U-shaped distribution of the relative power of adolescents in the family. Adolescents report having the least say in the middle of their teenage years. In general, relationships with parents are described as more unilateral than relationships with friends, which are essentially egalitarian. Considering an age-range from 12 years to 30 years, findings concerning relative power as measured by Furman and Buhrmester suggest a steady increase of young people's influence in the family well beyond the age of maturity. However, a balance of power is still not achieved between parents and their offspring in early adulthood (Noack, 1995).

Further confirmation of predictions derived from individuation theory is provided by results on the socio-emotional quality of family relationships (e.g., Claes, 1994; Larson & Richards, 1991; van Hekken, de Mey, Schulze, & Sinnige, 1994). While sound bonds between parents and their adolescent sons and daughters prevail, mostly U-shaped distributions were observed depending on age. Mirroring the patterns concerning authority and power, the quality of relationships reaches its low at mid-adolescence. It must be kept in mind that even in this age-group, the data suggest high levels of connectedness in absolute terms (cf. Furman & Buhrmester, 1992). Again, friendship relationships are described in more favorable terms. The highest rates of parent–adolescent conflicts roughly coincide with the peak of pubertal development. Several authors interpret this association as causal (cf. Steinberg, 1987). It seems plausible to assume that the perception of physical changes triggers or fosters adolescents' push for autonomy as well as parental attempts to stay in control; this could also explain reports of heightened unilateralness of relationship at mid-adolescence.

The evidence presently available clearly support notions of individuation theory. While a confound between age-specific trends and cohort effects in these studies, which examine relatively short intervals, is unlikely, it must be kept in mind that these findings are based on cross-sectional data. Furthermore, the self-report nature of the data limits our view of this process. Observational studies providing insights into the actual interactions between adolescents and their parents are rare.

PARENT–ADOLESCENT INTERACTIONS

At first glance, the importance of micro-level analyses of family interactions lies in the validity of self-report data. Some findings (e.g., Noack, 1993) suggest that relationship perceptions and behavioral data should not be considered interchangeable approaches to the same theoretical constructs. It may be conceptually more appropriate to proceed on the assumption of reciprocal influences linking family members' perceptions and behaviors. Unfortunately, individuation theory is not very precise in postulating age-specific changes of interactional behavior as well as changes in parents' and adolescents' social cognition. Independent of this theoretical question, however, parallel patterns of findings should be expected.

The research programs conducted by Grotevant and Cooper (e.g., Grotevant & Cooper, 1985, 1986) and Hauser, Powers, Noam, and colleagues (e.g., Hauser, Powers & Noam, 1991; Hauser, Powers, Noam, Jacobson, Weiss, &

Follansbee, 1984) have played a leading role in the study of family interactions at adolescence. In their analyses of families' interactions elicited by a planning task, Cooper, Grotevant, and Condon (1983) employed a coding system drawing on their conceptualization of family individuation during adolescence. The aggregate codes of mutuality, permeability, self-assertion, and separateness were designed to capture aspects of individuation in a differentiated way. While the findings provided instructive insights into the workings of interactions between adolescents and their parents and into associations between interactional behavior and aspects of adolescents' individual development, the studies did not address age-specific variations. Hauser et al. (1984) analyzed family discussions of moral dilemmas—a more conflictual type of interaction than that used by Cooper, Grotevant, and Condon (1983). Even though a different coding system (e.g., Powers, 1982) was employed in this research, there is some overlap of the basic codes and those developed by Grotevant and Cooper. Again, however, there is little information on variation in family members' behavior depending on adolescents' age.

One exception is provided in a study by Powers and Welsh (1993). The longitudinal findings are in line with the assumption that adolescents attempt to gain higher levels of autonomy with age. Allen, Hauser, O'Connor, Bell, and Eickholt (1996) provide another longitudinal study of interactional behavior during adolescence. Analyses of the stability of observed behaviors yielded small to moderate correlations across a two-year time interval. Longitudinal associations varied depending on the family member in focus as well as on the type of behavior analyzed. Concerning hostile moves family members showed in their interactions, for instance, correlations ranged between .17 and .42. Given the lack of other comparable studies, conclusive evidence for the postulated transformation of family relationships during adolescence is lacking.

THE EARLY ADOLESCENCE STUDY

The major objective of the study reported in the following is descriptive. We set out to examine patterns of family interactions and their changes in the course of early adolescence. Assessments of this two-year longitudinal study started when adolescents were about 13 years of age, a time when marked changes in cognitive and physical development impact family relations (Steinberg, 1993). Hormonal changes affecting adolescents' behavior, as well as the pubertal growth spurt and the development of secondary sex characteristics, can be assumed to influence the way family members perceive and respond to each other.

Even though observations of adolescents' interactions with their best friends were carried out in addition to assessments of family communication, the major focus of this chapter is on the family. Still, information on behavior in the friendship relationship can be drawn upon as background information contributing to a better understanding of the structure and micro-processes of family interactions. Moreover, we will mainly report on interactions elicited by a plan-something-together task (Grotevant & Cooper, 1985). Additional observational data based on a second task administered at each assessment (e.g., revealed differences paradigm) are available. The data provide some insights into the possible dependence of observed interactional behaviors on a specific situation.

With regard to tenets of individuation theory, we want to address two main areas of discussion. The first refers to the symmetric or asymmetric nature of behavior in family interactions. We expect a clearly asymmetric distribution of interactional behaviors of family members reflecting the dominant role of parents at early adolescence. At the same time, adolescents' thrust toward more autonomy should show up in comparably high rates of confrontational moves on the part of sons and daughters. Secondly, we aim at analyzing changes in family members' behavior during the years under study. Parental control as well as adolescents' challenges should increase, indicating an intensified negotiation of mutual perceptions and roles in the family.

Method

Analyses are based on data from 26 families who participated in interactions at each of the three measurements, which were conducted at yearly intervals. At first measurement, adolescents were 12.9 years of age (t2: 13.8; t3: 14.7) and attended the highest track of the German school system. As the institutionalized tracks of German schools roughly reflect socio-economic background, the participating families mostly share a middle to upper middle class status. Adolescents' parents were in their early 40s (t1, mothers: 41.0; fathers: 44.1).

As part of more comprehensive assessments conducted at the family homes, family members were given a planning task that elicited discussions lasting about 15 minutes. At first measurement, families were asked to plan activities for a weekend they were to spend together. In the following years, discussions focused on a family vacation and the question of what to do with a considerable amount of money won in a lottery, respectively. Audiotapes of the interactions were transcribed literally and coded on a turn-by-turn basis.

The coding followed an instrument introduced by Powers (1982) which provides 24 basic codes. It was developed for the analysis of discussions of moral dilemmas. The application to the planning situation required some minor changes. However, changes did not affect the basic structure of the original instrument. Changes occurred, for instance, for the differentiation of a given category or if existing categories had to be collapsed because of extremely low empirical frequencies. The resulting codes were aggregated into eight main codes: question, information (statements of facts or opinions), simple agreement, directive (requests or management of conversation), challenges (e.g., critique, counter-opinion, rejection), conflict (moves expressing negative affect), support (moves expressing positive affect), and justification. Tests of interrater agreement yielded results comparable to those reported for the original instrument (for more detailed information on codes, coding procedure, and reliabilities see Eichler, Fingerle & Noack, 1993).

Verbal Behavior in Family Interactions at Early Adolescence

Overall, patterns of behaviors were in line with the assumption of sound bonds between family members. Informational statements were clearly most frequent, followed by questions, simple agreements, and challenges. Confrontational moves expressing negative affect, namely aggressive utterances, were quite rare. It has to be kept in mind, however, that joint planning in the family is likely to elicit a sober and matter-of-fact atmosphere. Cooper, Grotevant, and Condon (1983), for instance, point out that planning tasks may accentuate mutuality and direct the focus of conversations toward shared views. Still, from our point of view, it is worth mentioning that supportive behaviors occurred about twice as often as conflictual moves.

Multivariate analyses of variance (MANOVA) with the eight types of behavior as dependent variables, measurement point (t1 - t3) and role in the family (son/daughter, father, mother) as within-subject factors, and adolescent gender as between-subject factor served to address our main research questions. For the sake of clarity, we do not report the various test statistics. Reference to systematic differences is based on statistically significant findings in MANOVAs and post hoc tests throughout the following, unless otherwise indicated.

As expected, there were several indications of asymmetric power relations in the family suggesting parental dominance. If we are right in considering questions as an indirect and gentle way of exerting control in interactions, it does not come as a surprise that parents asked more questions than did their sons and daughters. This is especially true of the maternal behavior. Likewise, parents often gave more directives. The number of questions asked in the interactions, however, decreased across time. As this change was more marked among the parents, initial differences had faded by the time of the third assessment. At the same time, parental directive behaviors increased. This could indicate intensified attempts at control that became more direct and explicit during the years under study. Figure 1 illustrates longitudinal changes in the relative frequencies of directives in the family communication.

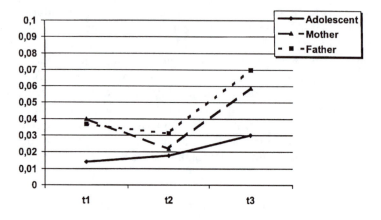

FIGURE 1.   Early Adolescence: Relative Frequencies of Directive Behaviors in Parent–Adolescent Interactions at Three Measurement Points.

The findings concerning confrontational behaviors also provide a differentiated picture. While there was no asymmetry in the distribution of challenges, adolescents showed more conflictual moves in the interactions than did their mothers. Even the frequency of mothers' challenging utterances decreased over time. Conversely, adolescents acted in an increasingly conflictual manner. This change was significant from second to third measurement; paternal conflict behavior also increased during this time. With fathers, however, the increase followed a substantial reduction of conflictual utterances during the first one-year interval. Even though this was also true for adolescents in absolute terms, the early decline of adolescent conflict behavior was not significant. The patterns of change are shown in Figure 2.

Again, the constellation of stable or even decreasing frequencies of challenges, on the one hand, and growing conflict, on the other, favors the view of an intensification of family negotiations in the course of early adolescence. It is less clear why paternal and adolescent conflict behaviors showed a U-shaped development. An interaction effect suggesting differential patterns of change in families with male and female adolescents is quite instructive in this respect. Whereas families with adolescent daughters showed more conflicts at first measurement than did families with sons, the opposite is true at third measurement. Thus, family conflicts seem to reach their peak at an earlier time in the former group—a finding that could be linked to the earlier onset of puberty among girls. With respect to the other behavioral codes, little systematic differences among family members or variation across time were observed.

A comparison of these findings with observations of the parallel planning interactions in adolescents' friendship dyads underscores the suggested in-

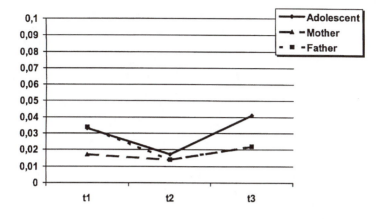

FIGURE 2.   Early Adolescence: Relative Frequencies of Conflict Behaviors in Parent–Adolescent Interactions at Three Measurement Points.

terpretations. With eight behavioral codes across three measurement points, there were only two instances of systematic differences between the behaviors of the target adolescents and their best friends. At second measurement, target adolescents contributed fewer statements of information to the conversation than their friends and showed a higher number of supportive moves. Friendship interactions were, thus, characterized by a high degree of symmetry. Analyses directly addressing target adolescents' behavior in both social contexts indicate, first, that adolescents were more confrontational in the family, showing higher frequencies of challenges and conflictual moves vis-à-vis their parents and, secondly, that they were comparably less dominant when interacting with their parents. Obviously, parental dominance offered less leeway for influencing the course of interaction—using questions or even directives—than possible in the egalitarian friendship situation.

These findings suggest that the Early Adolescence Study, indeed, captured the initial phase of family individuation. There were several instances of asymmetry in interactional behaviors, indicating parental dominance. At the same time, a comparably high share of adolescents' conflictual utterances can be seen as an attempt to resist control by fathers and mothers. A growing number of conflictual exchanges as well as increases of parental directive behaviors confirm the expected intensification of negotiations, which individuation theory considers the mechanism that eventually brings about the postulated transformation of family relations. On the first glance, decreases in the number of questions and challenges contradict this understanding. In light of the other findings, this pattern does rather point to a shift from more indirect to more direct modes of control and confrontation than to a decreasing intensity of discussions.

THE LATE ADOLESCENCE STUDY

The Late Adolescence Study can be considered a continuation of the work reported above. Family discussions elicited by planing tasks were observed at three measurement points starting when the adolescent sons and daughters were about 15 years old. At third assessment they had nearly reached age 17. Following individuation theory, the proposed transformation of family relations should have been carried quite far by this age. Consequently, we expect a decreasing intensity of negotiations as well as clear indications of more egalitarian patterns of interaction. Considerable differences between the samples of both studies and the coding systems employed, however, suggest caution when comparing the respective findings.

Method

The Late Adolescence Study was conducted as part of a more extensive investigation of associations between experiences of social change, family relations, and adolescents' individual development during the time after German unification. A major research question addressed young people's transition from school to work. For this reason, particular interest was paid to those adolescents attending 9th grade of middle track schools in East and West Germany. These boys and girls are confronted with the decision to enter work-life soon, start an apprenticeship, or continue school education. In order to arrive at a more detailed understanding of family processes in this group, we conducted behavioral observations in a small subsample of middle track students and their parents.

Presently, interactional data from the first three measurement points are available for a total of 47 families. About two-thirds of the families are living in an urban area of West Germany, one third is from a larger East German city. At first measurement, East and West German adolescents attended the 9th grade of middle track schools (mean ages: 14.6 and 14.9 years). Reflecting regional differences in ages of first child-bearing, East German parents were clearly younger (mothers: 39.2; fathers: 40.4) than were West German parents (mothers: 40.8; fathers: 44.6). Again, the sample is quite homogeneous, representing lower middle class to middle class backgrounds.

Behavioral observations and questionnaire assessments were conducted in the homes of the families. The instructions given at each of the three measurement points asked family members to plan a joint vacation, to decide the distribution of money won in a lottery, and to discuss how to proceed when the father—in the case of unemployment—is offered a job at a distance that would not allow daily commuting. Audiotapes of the 10-minute discussions were transcribed literally and coded using the coding scheme developed by Condon, Cooper, and Grotevant (1984). The instrument offers five codes to capture different functions of "moves" (e.g., direct suggestion, request) in interactions, seven "response" codes (e.g., indirect challenge/disagreement), and two additional categories ("other"; relevant comment, mindreading). Each meaningful unit is coded as to its "move" and "response" function. The assignment of an "other" code is optional. As no revisions were made for our purposes, readers are referred to the original manual (Condon et al., 1984) for details of the codes and coding procedure. Preliminary analyses did not confirm the four aggregate codes suggested in the manual ("mutuality," "permeability," "self assertion," "separateness"). Hence this study considers only the basic codes.

Verbal Behavior of Adolescents and Their Parents in Family Interactions

As in the Early Adolescence Study, MANOVAs and post hoc tests served to examine changes in interactional behavior across time as well as differences between family members. Again, we do not report individual coefficients. Variations indicated in the text refer to significant results of the statistical analyses.

A closer look at the distribution of interactional behaviors depending on the role in the family reveals asymmetric as well as symmetric aspects. Asymmetry prevailed with regard to control over the course of the conversation. While parents, namely mothers, asked more questions than adolescents did, adolescents contributed more answers to the conversations than their mothers (and fathers at t3). Moreover, higher frequencies of adolescents'—as compared to fathers'—acknowledgments confirm the impression of responsiveness on the parts of sons and daughters. In general, the frequency of questions decreased across time while acknowledgments increased. While these changes did not affect differences in acknowledgments between adolescents and their fathers, they resulted in more symmetry concerning questions in the family interaction. Still, a higher total number of parental utterances and relevant comments, in particular, adds to the interpretation of a slight dominance of mothers and fathers throughout the years in focus. This pattern of adolescent behavior may, however, reflect a slow withdrawal from the family as sons and daughters shed their submissive roles in interactions.

Another variation, depending on the role in the family, could be observed in mindreading behaviors. We prefer the term "mindreading" to "states other's feelings" as suggested by Condon et al. (1984), as it better expresses the implicit dominance inherent in statements about the thoughts and emotions of others. Indeed, mindreading was more frequent among mothers and fathers than among adolescents. For both parents, however, the frequency of mindreading declined across measurement points, resulting in a largely even distribution by the time of the third assessment. Figure 3 shows the changes of relative frequencies of adolescent, paternal, and maternal mindreading.

Differential patterns of change were also identified with regard to indirect suggestions. A decline of relative frequencies only occurred among adolescents. As a consequence, sons and daughters made a smaller number of indirect suggestions than their mothers at third measurement. Finally, there were some changes not linked to the role in the family. Direct and indirect disagreements became less frequent. Even though post hoc analyses suggest differential decreases (direct disagreement: mothers, adolescents; indirect disagreement: mothers, fathers), interaction effects of measurement point and role in the family remained insignificant. Likewise, an increase of agreements was mainly due to changes in paternal behavior without resulting in a significant interaction effect.

Our analyses did not provide any evidence for gender-specific variations. Differences between families in East and West Germany were not tested, as there were no plausible reasons to expect regional variations. Moreover, considering region as an independent variable would have resulted in very small cell sizes.

Summarizing in our investigation of family interactions during late adolescence, a good deal of symmetry between parental and adolescent behavior was observed. This is particularly true for directive behaviors and open confrontations as reflected by direct or indirect disagreements and challenges. Given the limitations of the coding scheme, we are not able to report on affective confrontations such as conflictual moves. Still, asymmetry was evident even in the late adolescent years with regard to more implicit aspects of influence exerted in conversations. Uneven distributions of ques-

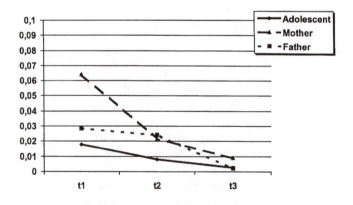

FIGURE 3. Late Adolescence: Relative Frequencies of Mindreading in Parent–Adolescent Interactions at Three Measurement Points.

tions, answers, and acknowledgments suggest a subliminal dominance on the part of the parents. It should be pointed out that this pattern gave way to an egalitarian situation concerning questions by the time adolescents had reached age 17. The same is true with respect to mindreading utterances, which we also interpreted as implicitly dominant. Moreover, increases of parental acknowledgments may also suggest that parents were starting to take the role of active listeners more seriously; that is, they behaved in a more reciprocal manner.

DISCUSSION

Taking individuation theory as our point of departure, we reported two longitudinal studies of behavior in interactions between adolescents and their parents. The age range addressed (13 to 17) is considered a period of the lifespan during which family relationships are transformed from unilateral control by parents toward more reciprocity and comparably egalitarian patterns. Protagonists of individuation theory claim that these changes cannot be brought about with fierce adolescent–parent conflicts. Rather they maintain that it requires a high level of connectedness, which facilitates the negotiation of new mutual perceptions and role patterns.

In a nutshell, our findings from microanalyses of family interactions favor tenets of individuation theory. While the overall level of fierce conflict and aggressive moves which we observed was low, there were clear indications of intensified negotiations between parents and their sons and daughters around mid-adolescence. Changes in family members' behaviors during the early adolescent years suggest a shift from indirect to more direct verbal means to arrive at the respective goals—namely, adolescents' moves toward increased autonomy and parental attempts not to lose control. At the same time, conflict and parental dominance remained low in absolute terms. Interactions during late adolescence provided some evidence for growing symmetry between adolescents and their parents, concerning subtle expressions of dominance in particular. These changes, however, were quite small, and the resulting situation was not fully egalitarian. Approaching the age of majority, adolescents still answered more questions of their parents than they asked. Likewise, sons and daughters' relative share of the interactions was smaller than their parents' contributions.

Summarizing, there was less indication of accomplished reciprocity in the families at late adolescence than expected, even though we observed some change in line with our hypotheses. These micro-analytic findings correspond to adolescents' self-reports describing family relations around majority (e.g., Noack, 1995). It may well be that around this time a new plateau of slight unilateralness in the family is reached that still favors the parents. The balance of power may change by the time young people move out of the family household and live on their own (Flanagan, Schulenberg, & Fuligni, 1993). Unfortunately, there is little empirical information on family relations during early adulthood and most of it refers to the lives of college students who experience a more dependent situation than do their age-mates in work-life (cf. Papastefanou, 1997). Still, some findings (Noack, 1995) suggest that parental dominance may not have faded until young people reach their late 20s.

Putting our findings into perspective, possible peculiarities due to the methodological approach chosen must be considered. It must be stressed again that the two studies reported in this chapter relied on different instruments. Consequently, differences between family members' behavior in early and late adolescence could be a methodological artifact. The lack of codes directly addressing the expression of positive or negative affect in the instrument of Condon et al. (1984) is a particularly noteworthy case in point. The possible impact of differences in more subtle shades of meaning of superficially similar codes, however, is more problematic. Our conclusions are, thus, clearly in need of further empirical support.

Also, we cannot rule out the possibility that the choice of interaction tasks influences the way parents and adolescents interact. In an early methodological study, Zuckerman and Jacob (1979) pointed out that differences in instructions, indeed, affect mean level of behavior in interactions. At the same time, however, structural properties of the interaction—such as the balance of power evidenced by behavioral asymmetry—showed considerable continuity across situations. Drawing on data of the Early Adolescence Study, our own analyses (Noack, 1997) corroborate this observation. Comparing the same family triads in the pursuit of a planning task and discussing a conflictual issue elicited by a revealed differences instruction, we found, for example, systematic variation in mean levels of behaviors. Differences in relative frequencies of directive and conflict behaviors are cases in point. Still, there were very few interaction effects involving instruction (planning, conflict discussion) and role in the family (adolescent, father, mother) which would indicate differential patterns of interaction, depending on the situation such as variation in dominance and submission.

Leaving aside these caveats and assuming some validity of our findings, a major challenge for future research will be to shed light on the processes responsible for the changes of family relations during adolescence. We proceeded on the assumption of reciprocal influences linking relationship transformation and adolescents' individual development. By now, considerable evidence has accumulated for effects of experiences in family interactions on adolescents' personality (e.g., Allen, Hauser, Bell, & O'Connor, 1994; Leaper et al., 1989). Clearly less is known concerning influences of the opposite direction. A major exception is the inquiry into the impact of puberty on family relations (e.g., Papini, Datan, & McCluskey-Fawcett, 1988; Steinberg, 1981). In our own data (Noack, 1995), we found some indication of circular processes linking adolescent self concept and behavioral autonomy, on the one hand, and behavior of adolescents and their parents in family interactions, on the other hand. A case in point is maternal challenges in the planning situation, which fostered adolescent self-efficacy. Higher levels of self-efficacy, in turn, resulted in increases of challenging behavior on the part of the mothers. Given the limitations of the study, further evidence addressing this model is clearly necessary. Research efforts aiming in this direction seem to be worthwhile, however, as a more thorough understanding of the processes involved should open ways to interrupt vicious instances of family and individual development and foster successful ones.

REFERENCES

Allen, J. P., Hauser, S. T., Bell, K. L., & O'Connor, T. G. (1994). Longitudinal assessment of autonomy and relatedness in adolescent–family interactions as predictors of adolescent ego-development and self-esteem. *Child Development, 65*, 179–194.

Allen, J. P., Hauser, S. T., O'Connor, T. G., Bell, K. L., & Eickholt, C. (1996). The connection of observed hostile family conflict to adolescents' developing autonomy and relatedness with parents. *Development and Psychopathology, 8*, 425–442.

Claes, M. (1994, February). *Adolescents' attachment to mother, father, and friends in three countries: Canada, Belgium, and Italy.* Poster presented at the Biennial Meetings of the Society for Research on Adolescence, San Diego, CA.

Collins, W. A., & Laursen, B. (1992). Conflict and relationships during adolescence. In C. U. Shantz & W. W. Hartup (Eds.), *Conflict in Child and Adolescent Development* (pp. 216–241). Cambridge, England: Cambridge University Press.

Condon, S. M., Cooper, C. R., & Grotevant, H. D. (1984). Manual for the analysis of family discourse. *Psychological Documents, 14*, 8 (Ms. 2616).

Cooper, C. R., Grotevant, H. D., & Condon, S. M. (1983). Individuality and connectedness in the family as context for adolescent identity formation and role-taking skill. *New Directions for Child Development, 22*, 43–58.

Eichler, A., Fingerle, M., & Noack, P. (1993). *Jugendgespraeche: Manual Kategorisierung* [Adolescent Conversations: Coding Manual]. Unpublished manuscript, University of Mannheim.

Flanagan, C., Schulenberg, J., & Fuligni, A. (1993). Residential setting and parent–adolescent relationships during the college years. *Journal of Youth and Adolescence, 22*, 171–189.

Furman, W., & Buhrmester, D. (1992). Age and sex differences in perceptions of networks of personal relationships. *Child Development, 63*, 103–115.

Grotevant, H. D., & Cooper, C. R. (1985). Patterns of interaction in family relationships and the development of identity exploration in adolescence. *Child Development, 56,* 415–428.

Grotevant, H. D., & Cooper, C. R. (1986). Individuation in family relationships: A perspective on individual differences in the development of identity and role-taking skill in adolescence. *Human Development, 29,* 82–100.

Hauser, S. T., Powers, S. I., & Noam, G. G. (1991). *Adolescents and Their Families.* New York: Free Press.

Hauser, S. T., Powers, S. I., Noam, G. G., Jacobson, A. M., Weiss, B., & Follansbee, D. J. (1984). Familial contexts of adolescent ego development. *Child Development, 55,* 195–213.

Hill, J. P. (1987). Research on adolescents and their families: Past and prospect. *New Directions for Child Development, 37,* 13–31.

Hofer, M., Klein-Allermann, E., & Noack, P. (Eds.). (1992). *Familienbeziehungen* [Family Relations]. Goettingen, Germany: Hogrefe.

Hofer, M., & Noack, P. (1992). *Individuation und sozialer Wandel* [Individuation and Social Change]. Antrag an die Deutsche Forschungsgemeinschaft, University of Mannheim.

Hofer, M., Noack, P., & Klein-Allermann, E. (1994). *Individuation und sozialer Wandel* [Individuation and Social Change]. Erster Fortsetzungsantrag an die Deutsche Forschungsgemeinschaft, University of Mannheim.

Hofer, M., Noack, P., Wild, E., & Kracke, B. 1996). *Individuation und sozialer Wandel* [Individuation and social change]. Zweiter Fortsetzungsantrag an die Deutsche Forschungsgemeinschaft, University of Mannheim.

Hunter, F. T. (1984). Socializing procedures in parent–child and friendship relations during adolescence. *Developmental Psychology, 20,* 1092–1099.

Leaper, C., Hauser, S. T., Kremen, A., Powers, S. I., Jacobson, A. M., Noam, G. G., Weiss-Perry, B., & Follansbee, D. (1989). Adolescent–parent interaction in relation to ego-development pathways: A longitudinal study. *Journal of Early Adolescence, 9,* 335–361.

Nave-Herz, R., & Markefka, M. (Eds.). (1989). *Handbuch der Familien- und Jugendforschung* [Family and Youth Research]. Neuwied, Germany: Luchterhand.

Noack, P. (1990). *Soziale Interaktion und Selbstkonzept im Jugendalter* [Social Interaction and Self Concept During Adolescence]. Antrag an die Deutsche Forschungsgemeinschaft, University of Mannheim.

Noack, P. (1991). *Untersuchung von Zusammenhaengen zwischen Aspekten des Selbstkonzepts und dem Umgang mit Eltern und Freunden* [Investigation into Aspects of the Self Concept and Interactions with Parents and Friends]. Fortsetzungsantrag an die Deutsche Forschungsgemeinschaft, University of Mannheim.

Noack, P. (1993). Zusammenhaenge zwischen Familieninteraktionen und Beziehungsqualitaeten aus Sicht der Familienmitglieder [Associations between behavior in family interactions and relationship quality as perceived by family members]. *Zeitschrift fuer Familienforschung, 5,* 115–133.

Noack, P. (1995). *Entwicklung naher Beziehungen im Jugendalter* [Development of Close Relationships During Adolescence]. Unpublished habilitation thesis, University of Mannheim.

Noack, P. (1997, September). *Interaktionsverhalten von Jugendlichen, Eltern und Freunden in Familien- und Freundschaftsgespraechen unter verschiedenen Instruktionsbedingungen* [Behavior of Adolescents, Parents, and Friends in Family and Friendship Interactions Depending on Task Instructions]. Paper presented at the Tagung Entwicklungspsychologie, Vienna, Austria.

Papastefanou, C. (1997). *Auszug aus dem Elternhaus* [Moving Out of the Family Home]. Weinheim, Germany: Juventa.

Papini, D. R., Datan, N., & McCluskey-Fawcett, K. A. (1988). An observational study of affective and assertive family interactions during early adolescence. *Journal of Youth and Adolescence, 17*, 477–492.

Pikowsky, B., & Hofer, M. (1992). Die Familie mit Jugendlichen. Ein Uebergang fuer Eltern und Kinder [The family with adolescents. A transition for parents and children]. In M. Hofer, E. Klein-Allermann & P. Noack (Eds.), *Familienbeziehungen* [Family Relations] (pp. 194–216). Goettingen, Germany: Hogrefe.

Powers, S. I. (1982). *Family Interaction and Parental Moral Development as a Context for Adolescent Moral Development*. Unpublished Ph.D. thesis, Harvard University.

Powers, S. I., & Welsh, D. (1993, March). *Changes in Family Interaction from Middle to Late Adolescence*. Paper presented at the Biennial Meetings of the Society for Research in Child Development, New Orleans, LA.

Steinberg, L. (1981). Transformations in family relations at puberty. *Developmental Psychology, 17*, 833–840.

Steinberg, L. (1987). The impact of puberty on family relations: Effect of pubertal status and pubertal timing. *Developmental Psychology, 23*, 451–460.

Steinberg, L. (1990). Autonomy, conflict, and harmony in the family relationship. In S. S. Feldman & G. Elliott (Eds.), *At the Threshold* (pp. 255–276). Cambridge, MA: Harvard University Press.

Steinberg, L. (1993). *Adolescence* (3rd ed.). New York: McGraw-Hill.

van Hekken, S. M. J., de Mey, L., Schulze, H.-J., & Sinnige, P. S. M. (1994). Kommunikationsstrukturen in Familien und mit Freunden—Bericht ueber eine Reihe von Projekten [Communication structures in family and friendship relations—Report on several studies]. *System Familie, 7*, 54–59.

Wilder, D. (1995). *Changes in Relationship Closeness, Reciprocity, and Authority During Adolescence*. Unpublished M.A. thesis, Florida Atlantic University.

Youniss, J., & Smollar, J. (1985). *Adolescent Relations with Mothers, Fathers, and Friends*. Chicago: University of Chicago Press.

Zuckerman, E., & Jacob, T. (1979). Task effects in family interaction. *Family Process, 18*, 47–53.

Chapter 6

Talk to Mom and Dad and Listen to What is in Between: A Differential Approach to Family Communication And its Impact on Adolescent Development*

Kurt Kreppner
Max-Planck Institute for Human Development and Education

Manuela Ullrich
Max-Planck Institute for Human Development and Education

INTRODUCTION

The family is an institution wherein children can learn to acquire social strategies, to solve problems, to express emotions, and to perceive and evaluate others as well as the relationships between them (Dunn, 1988). Through a long and enduring process, parents and children learn to adapt to one another. The daily encounters with others in the family—parents, siblings, or grandparents—constitute the basis for the child's first impression of how families interact, which creates recurring patterns of social behavior and modes of communication. These experiences can be taken as

* Scoring and data analysis of parent–parent communication were supported and financed by the Deutsche Forschungsgemeinschaft.

83

a basic framework for the child's expanding concepts of social relationships, the belief in the possibility that he or she can affect things and persons, and a growing sense of self.

This framework is established in ways parents communicate with children and each other. The impact of socialization activities in the family differs considerably across development. For example, during the first two or three years after birth, parents have to find a new rhythm for their own lives and to work on their views of how children's development should be influenced. The family's constitution is a first critical period when changes of relationships are necessary. Coping with these changes is considered an accomplishment of "family tasks" (Duvall, 1977) in analogy with Havighurst's (1953) concept of "developmental tasks." During critical periods in family development, members negotiate, revalue, reconstruct, and interpret transformations in everyday discussions.

When children during stable phases of their development do not show major deviations from expected behaviors, open regulations of rules and conflicts about the child's proper conduct normally remain at a minimum level. However, during periods of developmental change, new needs and demands have to be integrated in the family's lifestyle and canon of rules. During these transition periods, the transmission of rules or threat of sanctions becomes a frequent issue as described by Reiss (1981).

The transition from childhood to adolescence is another period of rapid changes with regard to body appearance, orientation to peers, and explorations outside the family. Parents have to adapt to the child's new demands and have to cooperate with each other to find a new way to integrate the adolescent into a common family life. Just as during toddlerhood, parents have to develop new skills in order to cope with the child's entrance to puberty.

In the present chapter, four major topics of family communication during the transition from childhood to adolescence will be addressed: Variation in parent–child and parent–parent communication modes, different modes of communication in parent–child dyads which can be linked to adolescents' differential assessments of the quality of relationship with the parent, and differences in parent–parent communications according to adolescents' differential ratings.

Mother–Child, Father–Child, Mother–Father–Child: The Establishing of a Family Perspective for Developmental Processes

The quality of the relationship between infants and parents became a salient issue during the late 1960s and 1970s when the reciprocal impact of parental influence on the child's development was regarded (Bell, 1968;

Escalona, 1973; Rheingold, 1969). Researchers began to differentiate stimulating from nonstimulating everyday interactions between parents and children in order to assess possible consequences for the development of cognitive and social skills. After a long period of studying mainly the mother–infant relationship, it was found that father absence reduced the well-being of babies. A series of studies documented the specific and important impact on children of father's behavior, for example, during play sessions (Lamb, 1975; Pedersen, 1975). Furthermore, evidence was also found that mother–child interaction changed in quality and quantity when the father was present. This, in turn, is also the case when father–child interaction is compared in presence or absence of the mother (Lewis & Feiring, 1978; Parke, 1979; Pedersen, Yarrow, Anderson, & Cain, 1978).

The above work was complemented by interest in the entire family encompassing the parent–parent and marital relationship (Pedersen, Anderson, & Cain, 1980). Belsky (1981) suggested a holistic strategy for family research that assumed mutual influences among father–child, mother–child, and marital relationships, thus incorporating the marital relationship into the network in which a child grows up. Therefore, aside from dyadic, also triadic interaction settings become the target of studies focusing on family influences on child development (Clarke-Stewart, 1978; McHale, 1995).

The importance of a secure attachment with the primary caretaker was another basic finding which changed popular thinking about children's development. Secure attachment during the first year is considered an important protective factor (Bowlby, 1969, 1973) that is facilitated by well-functioning interactions between mother or father and child. Longitudinal studies have shown that secure attachment is associated with children's abilities to explore, to develop social skills, to display fewer problems outside the home, and to achieve higher academic achievement (Mayseless, 1996; Van Ijzendoorn, 1996). Longitudinal studies over 20 years (Beckwith, Cohen, & Hamilton, 1995; Hamilton, 1994; Waters, Merrick, Albersheim, & Treboux, 1995; Zimmermann, 1994) indicate that quality of attachment is linked to stability in the family interaction climate, mainly with the ability to cope with stressful situations. With the Adult Attachment Interview (AAI) (George, Kaplan, & Main, 1984), a new approach could be established to gain information about an adult's attachment status by a retrospective interview technique. Under a family socialization perspective, it appears to be of major interest to compare, for instance, both parents' attachment status with the child's quality of attachment. As Steele, Steele, and Fonagy (1996) have found, links exist between parents' AAI classifications and their children's attachment quality assessed by the strange situation procedure. Thus, children's behaviors and the likelihood to follow different pathways in their own development appear to be influenced by the parents' adult attachment quality, the parents' abilities to cope with stressful situations, and to maintain the stability of family climate.

The Role of Marital Relationship in a Child's Development in Infancy and Early Childhood

Considerable evidence shows that marital functioning is important for a child's course of development. According to Parke and Buriel (in press), development of children's antisocial behavior (Emery, 1982), internalization problems (Katz & Gottman, 1993), and emotional and cognitive responses to marital conflict (Cummings & Davies, 1994; Gottman & Katz, 1989) have proven ties to the influential power of the quality of marital relationships. In a longitudinal approach, Cowan and Cowan (1987, 1988, 1992; Cowan, Cowan, Heming, & Miller, 1991) found that the quality of the marital relationship was a crucial factor for both parents' and the child's well-being during the transition period from being a couple to parenthood. The higher the quality of the marital relationship during pregnancy, the better the couple's ability to cope with stress during the first months after birth. Moreover, a meta-analysis conducted by Erel and Burman (1995) revealed that a direct influence exists between the quality of the marital relationship and a child's relationship with the parents, indicating transfer between one subsystem in the family (parent–parent dyad) to another (parent–child dyad). However, when moderators of this transfer are debated, no consistent results could be found.

Differences between mothers' and fathers' parenting styles gave new insights into possible consequences for the child's development when confronted with two instead of only one parent model. It is not the difference between styles but the parents' mutual support and acceptance of their different ways of handling the child that appears to be important. Belsky, Crnic, and Gable (1995) demonstrated that a consistent and supportive pattern of coparenting proved to be a relevant aspect for children's coping ability. Children between the ages of 2 and 5, whose parents have a strained relationship, express concern and tend to comfort their mothers when confronted with conflictual discourse between their mother and a strange person, whereas children with parents with a non-strained relationship exhibit less frequent strong reactions (Cummings, J.S., Pellegrini, Notarius, & Cummings, E.M., 1989). In two other studies children and adolescents were asked to imagine possible endings to conflictual episodes between parents. Hostile or ambivalent endings produced more emotional involvement in children than did harmonious endings (Davies, Myers, & Cummings, E. M., 1996; Shifflett-Simpson & Cummings, E. M., 1996). Furthermore, patterns of emotion regulation between parents or between parents and children predicted children's behavior in the classroom (Boyum & Parke, 1995). Belligerence and hostility during parents' discussions predicted children's externalization tendencies, whereas withdrawal and emotional distance during parental discussions was associated with children's inclination to internalize (Katz & Gottman, 1993).

These studies show that parents' communication styles affect children's emotional involvement and also are relevant for their experiencing an inner representation of the parent–parent relationship. Reasons for this link, however, are not clearly understood.

Only a few studies have directly addressed the importance of the marital relationship for the child's further development into adulthood. For example, in a cross-sectional large sample, Olson and McCubbin (1983) presented marital and family satisfaction rating of couples at different stages of the family life cycle. Marital satisfaction declined for mothers and fathers during children's puberty but rose dramatically after children had left home. Under a family perspective, parent–parent communication could be taken as a kind of stage-determining example in the child's many rehearsals to perform his or her own new role in the family. In a recent longitudinal study, Feldman, Fisher, and Seitel (1997) have shown that marital satisfaction during the child's adolescence was an important predictor of subsequent emotional and physical health of children six years later. It can be assumed that a family's framework for interpretation, which is produced by the specific modes of communication between members, has an important impact on both individual well-being and personality development also during the transition period from childhood to adolescence (Silverberg, 1996; Silverberg & Steinberg, 1990). Elements of conversations in the family, such as challenging statements or supporting or discouraging remarks, exert major influence on adolescents' self representations (Grotevant & Cooper, 1986; Hauser, Powers, & Noam, 1991). As family-specific communication styles tend to keep their format across situations (Keppler, 1994), differences in the families' ways to produce meaning may provide extremely valuable information on the children's and adolescents' potential development (Youniss, 1983, 1989; Youniss & Smollar, 1985).

FROM CHILDHOOD TO ADOLESCENCE IN THE FAMILY, AN EMPIRICAL EXAMPLE: DIFFERENCES IN COMMUNICATION SCENARIOS DURING A TRANSITION PERIOD

Aims, Design, and Selected Results of the Study

In a longitudinal study (Kreppner, 1995, 1996), continuity and change of parent–child communication were explored during the transition from childhood to adolescence and linked to adolescents' self-development. Effects of parent–parent communication were also examined and linked to adolescents' self development (Kreppner & Ullrich, 1997). The study focused on the observation of both parent–adolescent and parent–parent communication in discussions about everyday topics. Sixty-seven children and their parents (from former West Berlin) were followed up for three and a half years; the children were about 11 years old at the beginning of the study and about 15 years old at the end of the study. One of the study's main aims was to analyze changes in communication patterns over time. Another aim was to analyze communication patterns in parent–child as well in parent–parent dyads according to different types of relationship quality assessed by the children. Gender and family status differences were explored and have been described elsewhere (Kreppner, 1995).

Questionnaires exploring the quality of adolescents' relationships with their parents as well as their self-assessments were administered from the beginning of the study in six-month intervals. The quality of the relationship with the parents encompasses three scales, two of which cover dependability and emotional ambivalence with father and mother separately (Spiel, Kreppner, & Von Eye, 1995) with items such as "I can talk really well with him/her about my daily experiences" for dependability and "Often I would like to give my dad/mom a hug, but I don't do it" for ambivalence. The intensity of discussion between child and mother was measured with an instrument developed by Robin and Weiss (1980) encompassing items such as, "During the last two weeks we had a lot of arguments about how I spend my free time."

These scales were analyzed with regard to possible differences in adolescents' answers according to gender, family structure (two-parent or single-parent), and age (less than 11 years and 6 months versus older for the first wave). No statistically significant overall differences were found. For further analysis of differences across adolescents in assessing the quality of relationship with their parents, a cluster analysis was conducted with the first wave data of adolescents' ratings (Ward, 1963). Three groups of adolescents were identified showing marked differences in the quality of relationship with both mother and father. The groups were described as *habitual, ambivalent,* and *secure.* According to the cluster-group profile, the habitual cluster group showed average dependability, low ambivalence, and low discussion intensity. The ambivalent cluster group expressed a much higher degree of ambivalence with both parents compared to the other two groups, average dependability, and discussion intensity. Finally, the secure cluster group was characterized by a high quality of dependability with both parents, very low ambivalence, and a high amount of discussion intensity with mothers.

In order to assess the predictive power of cluster membership for later periods, hierarchical regression analyses were carried out. Included in the regression analysis as independent variables were gender, age of adolescents, and family status. In the second step cluster membership during the first wave was assessed for dependability, ambivalence, and discussion intensity during the fourth, sixth, and eighth wave of data collection. Results indicated that adolescents' ratings of both dependability and ambivalence during the fourth, sixth, and eighth wave could be predicted by adolescents' cluster membership during the first wave.

Two major groups of hypotheses were formulated: We expected, in line with Hill (1987), an increase of communication formats indicating dissent between the generations when the child reaches the age of 13 years and a kind of consolidation thereafter. A similar trend was expected in the nonverbal display of distance or closeness during discussions between parents and children. A second area of hypotheses pertained to children's estimations of the quality of family relationships. Exchange of opinions was assumed to occur more frequently in the secure than in the ambivalent group. A reduced rate of activity in discussions (increased silence) was believed to occur in ambivalent adolescents' communication behavior. A mixed pattern was hypothesized for parents' communication behavior when talking with their adolescent children. Guidance in discussions (clear statements about own opinions) was expected for both mothers and fathers whose children had rated a secure relationship quality, whereas affirmative behavior was expected from mothers from the ambivalent adolescents and a kind of neutral or disengaged communication behavior was hypothesized for fathers from this cluster group.

As to the nonverbal aspect of communication, a differential pattern for the regulation of closeness and distance across time was expected for the three cluster groups. In the secure cluster group, both parents and the adolescent were supposed to display higher rates of closeness. For the communication between both parents without the child present, neither time nor cluster-group variations were expected.

Discussion behavior in family dyads: Observation and coding procedure

Discussion situations between husbands and wives as well as between parents and children were recorded. Each dyad had to discuss a number of statements printed on stimulus cards such as (for parent–parent dyad): "Imagine you wake up one morning and are 17 years old again but with today's knowledge. How would you plan your life?" or, (for the parent–adolescent dyad), "Some in the family do not clean up their room as they should." Each topic was discussed for about two minutes. For the discussions, 10 cards per dyad and family were given in the first wave, five cards per dyad were given in the fourth, sixth, and eight wave. Topics on cards varied over time, and each topic appeared only once during the entire period. Families were observed while discussing in dyads (mother–child, father–child, mother–father) in four of the eight waves of data collection, when the child was 11.6, 13, 14, and 15 years old (first, fourth, sixth, and eighth wave). With these four observations, the entire range of the three-and-a-half year transition period was covered. Four trained coders processed the videotapes; they were blind with regard to families' social background or other characteristics such as family status. Coders scored the cards on an event basis. Each discussion following the reading of a card was taken as one event and served as the scoring unit. The categories used to describe the discussions had been specified after a series of pilot observations. For each dyad all cards were scored before coders moved on to the next dyad. The discussion of each card was coded in regard to a number of different categories.

In the following description we refer to the results of only two categories: *communication style*, with the levels "statement," "giving attention," "negotiation," "silence" (for adolescents) and "teaching" (for parents); and *closeness* with the four levels "very low," "low," "high," and "very high." These two categories represent dissimilar but essential aspects of dyadic communication according to the differentiation between "digital" (verbal) and "analogue" (nonverbal) messages contained in any information exchanged by persons (Watzlawick, Beavin, & Jackson, 1967). This selection of communication aspects renders a somewhat abridged but concise version of a family's "communication culture." "Communication style" refers to offers coming from a discussion partner to begin a discussion or to keep a discussion going. The levels describe whether the dialogue partner affirmed his or her own position without being sensitive to the other's view (statement), whether he or she was attentive and open to the other's talk (giving attention), whether the dialogue partner directed the other (parent–child) or denied the offers of silence (child–parent) or, finally, whether both partners offered opinions and tried to come to a common solution (negotiation). The category of "closeness" registers a different and nonverbal aspect of a family's communication climate. The exhibition of "high" or "low" closeness is believed to signal a family's capability of expressing feelings and dealing with the regulation of distance among family members. During the period of transition from childhood to adolescence, this regulation of distance is believed to be at stake in many families and a vital topic of negotiations between parents and children.

Reliabilities for these categories were obtained by computing kappa coefficients for two raters who had coded all categories for each event independently of each other (Cohen's Kappas ranged from .63 to .78 for the two selected variables in the different dyads. Details of cards, data collection procedure, scoring, categories, and statistical data analysis are given in Kreppner and Ullrich, 1996).[1] Frequency distributions for each of the categories were arranged in three dimensional cross-tabulations (see Fienberg

1980; Von Eye, Kreppner, & Wessels, 1992, 1994; Wickens, 1989) by crossing the variables Time [T], Cluster Membership [C], and Observed Level of a Category [O]. Changes over time as well as frequency variations according the different cluster membership were of major interest. Models with a probability greater .05 were selected as fitting for explaining the frequency patterns found in the respective cross-tabulations.[2] Models with interaction terms including observed levels of communication and time [TO], observed levels of communication and cluster membership [CO], or saturated models (with a triple interaction term [COT]) were analyzed according to the significance of the parameter estimates which were computed for the selected models.

Analysis of classified communication behavior in family dyads

As Table 1 indicates, log-linear analyses of the two selected categories "communication style" and "closeness" for all three dyads convey a rather complex pattern of different models. As each variable has been scored for both dyad partners separately, the resulting 12 models reveal a difference in complexity of the models.

Models found to describe the frequency patterns in the various cross-tabulations for the communication behaviors in the families' different dyadic constellations showed that, with only one exception, cluster member-

TABLE 6.1. Log-Linear Models for Categories "Communication Style" and "Closeness" in Three Family Dyads

	Model	p
Dyad Adolescent–Mother		
Communication style mother	saturated	
Communication style adolescent	saturated	
Closeness mother	[CO], [TO]	.42
Closeness adolescent	[CO], [TO]	.75
Dyad Adolescent–Father		
Communication style father	saturated	
Communication style adolescent	[C], [TO]	.30
Closeness father	[CO], [TO]	.11
Closeness adolescent	saturated	
Dyad Mother–Father		
Communication style mother	[CO], [TO]	.42
Communication style father	[CO], [TO]	.37
Closeness mother	[CO], [TO]	.08
Closeness father	[CO], [TO]	.26

ship of children accounted for specific communicative behavior in parent–child as well as in parent–parent discussions. As can be seen from the table of models, the terms [CO] or [COT] (for saturated models) were necessary in 11 out of 12 cases to explain the frequency distributions. Whereas the model with the double dyadic interaction term [CO], [TO] prevailed in the parent–parent communication, it appeared two times in the mother–adolescent and only once in the father–adolescent dyads. The saturated model is adequate to describe distributions found for the communication style in the mother–adolescent dyad and father's communication style with their children and children's closeness when discussing with their fathers. The saturated model signifies a high degree of complexity in the mutual influences of time, cluster membership, and mode of communication. The most parsimonious model, [C], [TO] appeared appropriate for describing the frequencies found for adolescents' communication style in the dyad with their fathers. This means that adolescents vary only over time and do not show cluster-specific differences in their communication with their fathers.

Time-Specific and Cluster-Specific Aspects of Communication in Family Dyads

By assessing parameter estimates for different contrasts in the cross-tabulation's dimensions, significant deviations for each of the levels in one category can be traced. We estimated parameters from contrast variables defined in a way similar to linear contrasts in ANOVAs (for details see Evers & Namboodiri, 1978; Rindskopf, 1990; Von Eye et al., 1992, 1994). For the models the parameters for the interaction terms [TO], [CO], as well as the triple interaction term [COT] appearing in the saturated models are of primary interest, as these terms detail variable interactions (see Tables 2 and 3).

In the following section, for both selected categories, communication style and closeness, the most relevant results in all three dyadic constellations (mother–adolescent, father–adolescent, and mother–father) will be interpreted according to the significant parameter estimates in the selected models (for technical details see Kreppner & Ullrich, 1996).

Communication style in different family dyads over time

Mothers' frequencies for "communication style" show a distribution that can only be described by a saturated model. This means that mothers, aside from displaying general variations over time and showing a pattern associated with cluster-membership, also exhibit a time-specific behavior according to the cluster membership of their children. The main tendencies are manifest in two major changes in mothers' behaviors toward their children over time: First, mothers increase their "statements" and "negotiations," es-

TABLE 2. Z-Transformed Parameter Estimates for "Communication Style"

Contrasts:

Time

wave 4 = contrast category
wave 1 – 4 = 1
wave 6 – 4 = 2
wave 8 – 4 = 3

Cluster Membership

cluster secure = contrast category
cluster habitual – secure = 1
cluster ambivalent – secure = 2

Communication Style

attention = contrast category
statement – attention = 1
teaching (p) – attention = 2
silence (a) – attention = 2
negotiation – attention = 3

Constellation cell	Father – Adolescent Model: saturated	Mother – Adolescent Model: saturated	Adolescent – Mother Model: saturated	Adolescent – Father Model: [C], [TO]	Mother – Father Model: [CO], [TO]	Father – Mother Model: [CO], [TO]
Time by Communication [TO]	z-value					
11	- 2.03*	- 1.09	- 3.41*	- .25	- 3.86*	- 4.25*
12	1.29	- 2.20	- 1.87	1.12	- 3.13*	- 2.32*
13	.96	.09	- 2.87*	2.76*	- 1.16	- .55
21	1.80	.07	1.46	.59	- 1.97*	- 1.77
22	1.71	.11	.39	.68	- 1.48	- 2.59*
23	3.34*	.88	- .16	2.27*	- .72	- .50
31	1.72	2.14*	.30	.47	- 2.40*	- 4.15*
32	.59	- 1.20	- .31	3.15*	- 1.46	- .34
33	2.88*	3.11*	.85	1.52	- .19	- 1.70

table continues

TABLE 2. (Continued)

Constellation	Father – Adolescent Model: saturated	Mother – Adolescent Model: saturated	Adolescent – Mother Model: saturated	Adolescent – Father Model: [C], [TO]	Mother – Father Model: [CO], [TO]	Father – Mother Model: [CO], [TO]
Cluster by Communication [CO]						
cell	z-value					
11	-2.02*	-.08	.55		3.18*	1.23
12	-1.41	.28	2.25*		.31	.95
13	.39	.54	-.85		1.48	3.30*
21	.17	-.19	-.41		.76	1.45
22	-.34	.97	2.06*		-.84	1.98*
23	.07	-.38	-.88		.47	2.19*
Time by Cluster by Communication [TCO]						
cell	z-value					
111	1.07	.08	-2.19*			
112	1.72	-1.11	.06			
113	-.97	-2.80*	-.64			
121	.39	2.04*	-1.95			
122	.77	.85	.59			
123	-.82	-1.60	-.06			
211	-2.17*	.11	-.53			
212	-2.01*	-.91	-.57			
213	-3.01*	-.91	1.23			
221	-1.83	.34	-1.60			
222	-1.35	-.16	-.09			
223	-2.31*	-.82	.47			
311	-1.60	-.11	1.05			
312	-.56	-.86	1.69			
313	-1.98*	-1.66	1.28			
321	-2.42*	-.01	.25			
322	-.57	.24	2.07*			
323	-2.06*	-.63	1.17			

TABLE 3. Z-Transformed Parameter Estimates for "Closeness"

Contrasts:

Time
wave 4 = contrast category
wave 1 – 4 = 1
wave 6 – 4 = 2
wave 8 – 4 = 3

Cluster Membership
cluster secure = contrast category
cluster habitual – secure = 1
cluster ambivalent – secure = 2

Closeness
low = contrast category
very low – low = 1
high – low = 2
Very high – low = 3

Constellation Father – Adolescent Model: [CO], [TO]	Mother – Adolescent Model: [CO],[TO]	Adolescent – Mother Model: [CO], [TO]	Adolescent – Father Model: saturated	Mother – Father Model: [CO], [TO]	Father – Mother Model: [CO], [TO]
Time by Closeness [TO]					
cell z-value					
11 -3.30*	2.42*	-.96	1.00	-3.34*	-2.75*
12 1.88	2.51*	2.81*	1.92	3.19*	4.08*
13 -.91	.95	.91	.11	.22	.95
21 -3.90*	.85	-.61	.15	.76	-.16
22 -.47	.87	.45	-1.18	1.76	2.13*
23 -1.85	-1.91	-1.82	-1.21	-.51	-.58
31 -3.62*	1.63	-.97	.65	-.09	-1.39
32 -.12	-.37	-.84	-.34	2.39*	1.83
33 -1.57	-.83	-2.02*	.27	-1.85	-1.55

table continues

TABLE 3. (Continued)

Constellation cell	Father – Adolescent Model: [CO], [TO] z-value	Mother – Adolescent Model: [CO],[TO]	Adolescent – Mother Model: [CO], [TO]	Adolescent – Father Model: saturated	Mother – Father Model: [CO], [TO]	Father – Mother Model: [CO], [TO]
Cluster by Closeness [CO]						
11	-3.08*	-1.00	2.34*	.91	1.66	-.66
12	2.50*	-.68	.16	2.04*	-.86	-1.57
13	-1.84	-3.02*	-3.19*	-1.00	-2.31*	-1.79
21	-2.04*	.90	2.12*	-.70	.89	.14
22	.24	-.80	1.56	2.43*	-1.14	-1.38
23	-4.64*	-3.36*	-2.68*	-3.42*	-3.10*	-2.99*
Time by Cluster by Closeness [TCO] z-value						
111				-1.25		
112				-.81		
113				-.39		
121				-1.09		
122				.09		
123				.41		
211				.62		
212				1.68		
213				1.16		
221				-.06		
222				1.87		
223				.63		
311				-.30		
312				-.31		
313				-1.47		
321				-2.01*		
322				.45		
323				.35		

pecially during the eighth wave when children are about 15 years old. Second, mothers decrease their activities concerning "teaching" and "giving attention" during the eighth wave. When mothers'communication styles are analyzed with regard to cluster membership and time period, a propensity of using "statments" already during the first wave, when children are about 11-and-a-half years old, is seen in dyads where adolescents have rated their relationship with parents as being ambivalent. Mothers of adolescents with a "secure" rating of their relationship negotiated more frequently, even in discussions during the first wave compared to the other two clusters. What becomes evident from these trends is that mothers change their discussion behavior at the end of the transition period, but not earlier. Results also indicated that adolescents' estimates of the quality of relationship with their parents have a concrete counterpart in mothers' communication behavior use of "statements" as an indicator of affirming one's own position without taking the partner into account, signals a more difficult discussion climate in dyads of the ambivalent compared to the secure group. Furthermore, mothers of the secure group "negotiate" with their children much earlier than mothers from the other two groups.

Adolescents' communication formats with their mothers generally display a sharp increase of "statement" and also "negotiation" during the fourth wave, when they reach 13 years of age. This mirrors adolescents' striving for autonomy and affirmation of their own position at an age which is the apex of adolescent development and pubertal crisis. Furthermore, cluster-specific differences in communication patterns indicate that adolescents from the ambivalent and the habitual cluster show "silence" more frequently in discussions than adolescents from the secure cluster, independently of time. At the stand of the transition period, the use of "statements" is less frequently in the ambivalent and habitual group compared to the secure group.

Fathers, like mothers, show a complex pattern of differential behavior in communication style with their children. Over time, fathers tend to use fewer statements in their discussions when children are still at the onset of their puberty (11–12 years), but they continuously stay at a lower "statement" level than mothers during the entire period. However, the frequency of negotiations in discussions with adolescents increase considerably after age 13. Cluster-specific differences are also manifest for fathers. Fathers whose children assess their relationship as being secure, show higher frequencies of "statement" compared to fathers from the habitual cluster group. When time-specified differences combined with cluster-specific differences are considered, a similar trend in the use of statements and negotiation is evident at the end of the observation period. Fathers from the ambivalent and habitual clusters give statements less frequently than fathers from the secure cluster.

Adolescents display a less complex pattern in their communication style with their fathers. According to the model [C], [TO], only differences over time characterize children's communication behavior. "Silence" is found more often during the end of the observation period, when adolescents reach the age of 15, whereas the use of negotiation occurs less frequently when children are 13 years old compared to earlier and later periods.

Overall, fathers exhibit a varied and rich picture of their communication modes with their children. At the children's age of 13, a remarkable shift in the use of paternal "statements" occurs over time. When cluster-specific differences are considered, fathers of adolescents from the secure group show increased engagement and affirmation of their own position already at the apex of their children's puberty and thereafter. Adolescents who have judged their relationship with their parents as being ambivalent or habitual experience fathers who, particularly when children are already beyond the apex of puberty, appear less active and more withdrawn.

Finally, when *marital* communication style in the dyad between husband and wife is analyzed, a general time-specific trend is salient for both parents. The use of "statement" increases dramatically during the fourth wave. "Silence" was less frequently found during the first wave compared with the fourth wave in both wives' and husband's behaviors. Thus, when their children reach the age of 13, parents' dyadic discussions show a high degree of affirmation when exchanging opinions or remain silent in reaction to the partner's contribution. When cluster-specific differences in communication style are considered, mothers of adolescents from the habitual cluster show more use of statements compared to mothers of adolescents from the secure cluster, and fathers of adolescents from both the habitual and ambivalent cluster display a significantly higher frequency of negotiation in marital communication compared to fathers of adolescents from the secure cluster. Aside from a clear sign of increased stress in all parental discussions during the fourth wave, a higher degree of arduous exchange of statements and long enduring negotiations seems to be typical in the dialogue of parents whose children have judged relationships with their parents as ambivalent.

Closeness in different family dyads over time
Nonverbal communication aspects and their changes over time are the second focus of this analysis. Low or high closeness among family members is taken as an indicator of a family's specific way to regulate distance and cope with the different members' changing needs and emotional states. General changes over time in closeness in parent–adolescent as well as in parent–parent interactions and cluster-specific difference patterns of closeness are considered (for a more intense illustration of an overall cluster-specific trend, differences across clusters with regard to the occurrence of "very high" closeness are depicted in Figures 1 to 3).

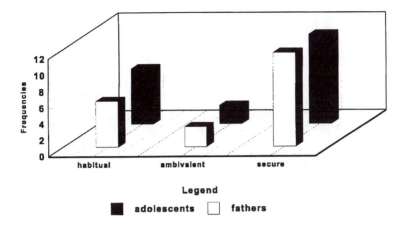

FIGURE 1. Clusterspecific Communication Patterns Very High Closeness: Fathers to Adolescents.

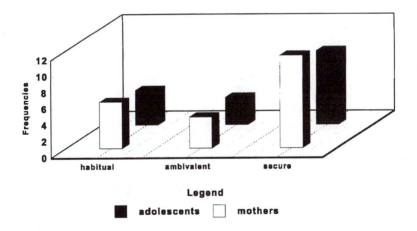

FIGURE 2. Clusterspecific Communication Patterns Very High Closeness: Mothers to Adolescents.

Mothers' closeness exhibits a time-specific trend which is in line with the expectation that a new balance between closeness and distance between parents and children has to be found during the period of puberty. Higher rates for high closeness occur more frequently during the first wave (children are 11–12 years old) compared to later waves. Cluster-specific differentiation is also found in mothers' display of closeness when talking with their children. In comparison to mothers from the secure cluster, mothers

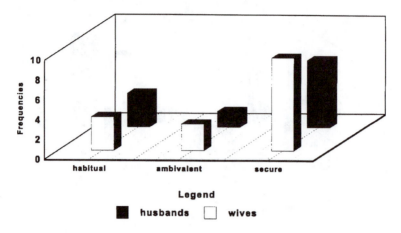

FIGURE 3. **Clusterspecific Communication Patterns Very High Closeness: Wives to Husbands.**

from habitual and ambivalent clusters exhibit significantly lower frequencies in expressing high closeness.

Adolescents who talk with their mothers produce a similar time-specific pattern by displaying high closeness during the first wave and a decrease of closeness thereafter. As to cluster-specific differences, low closeness is found more often in adolescents from the habitual and ambivalent cluster group than the secure cluster.

Fathers also exhibit a time-specific pattern of closeness. Low closeness in father–child dyads occurs most frequently when children reach the age of 13. High levels of closeness are found more often in dyads in which adolescents rated their relationship with fathers as "habitual," whereas fathers of adolescents who had rated the relationship as being "ambivalent" exhibit lower frequencies for very high closeness compared to fathers from the secure cluster. Fathers from the secure cluster who are intermediate give a rich example of varying the closeness–distance regulation, which leaves enough space for the child to find his or her own way to establish a new balance with the parents.

Adolescents in their discussions with fathers display more prominent differences across the three cluster groups than general changes across time. Closeness in adolescents' communication with their fathers is more frequently found in adolescents from the habitual and ambivalent cluster groups than in adolescents from the secure cluster group. Secure adolescents show a more distant behavior. However, when the few frequencies of the level "very high" are regarded, adolescents from the secure group showed this characteristic more often than adolescents from the ambivalent cluster. When cluster-specific differences were considered over time, another detail of divergent dialogical behaviors was revealed: Compared to the other two groups, adolescents from the secure cluster show both "very high" and "very low" closeness more frequently. These results imply that *variety* in the realization of a communication climate allows changes and space for regulation of the closeness–distance balance. This variety in behavior is associated with high quality judgment by the adolescents concerning the relationships with the parents.

The analysis of *marital* closeness reveals a time-specific trend which covaries with the child's developmental progress during puberty. High closeness in *wives'* discussions with their husbands is observed more frequently during the first and eighth wave and less frequently during the fourth wave. Low closeness is found rarely during the first wave compared to the fourth wave. These results complement each other as a general time-specific pattern describing fluctuations in wives' marital communications. There is also a clear trend pointing to a cluster-specific differentiation in parents' marital discussions with very high closeness in marital communication occurring less frequently in mothers of adolescents from both the habitual and the ambivalent compared to the secure cluster.

A similar pattern of closeness appears when *husbands* communicate with their wives. There is a time-specific fluctuation of displaying closeness between the first and the sixth wave. High frequencies for the expression of high closeness is found for husbands during the first and sixth wave, but not during the fourth wave, when children reach the age of 13. Corresponding to wives' closeness in dyads with their husbands, low closeness is also rarely found in husbands' behavior during the first wave, but more frequently thereafter. Thus, marital communication exposes an increase in "very low" closeness as well as large decrease in "high" closeness during the apex period of puberty. Finally, fathers of adolescents from the ambivalent cluster reveal generally a lower amount of "very high" closeness as compared to fathers of adolescents from the secure cluster.

DISCUSSION

The Role of Parent–Parent Discussions as a Model for the Children to Test and Explore New Formats of Communication

A major result of the study is that adolescents' differential ratings of the quality of relationship were linked to variations of communication behaviors found in different parent–child dyads over time and to differences in marital communication patterns. Adolescents grouped according to their relationship judgments as "habitual," "ambivalent," or "secure" obviously experience different communication situations in family dyads, and parents, when talking with each other, produce different communication patterns. Parents of adolescents from the "secure" cluster, for example, show a higher degree of agreement when exchanging opinions and displaying higher closeness when nonverbal aspects of interpersonal communication are regarded. Seen from the eyes of a child, this may generate a different atmosphere in the family compared to what children from the other two groups experience when watching their parents try to solve a problem. It was found in our longitudinal study that a family's "communication culture" is manifest in all dyads and is not restricted to intergenerational dyads. The adolescent experiences in parents' communication a model for potential critical negotiations with his or her parents. Thus, the notion of "communication culture" seems adequate to describe a family's overarching principles how via communication, the relationships among members are defined and information is shared (Burgess, 1926).

A Perspective on Family Communication Emphasizing its Function for the Child's Mastering of Developmental Transitions

In both verbal and nonverbal communication, the everyday small talk about mundane issues is of major interest when a period of transition such as the passage from childhood to adolescence has to be mastered in the family. When one thinks about such a period and the developmental tasks associated with it, one should take into account that the entire family has to cope with increased stress in *all* its relationships. As this is the case after the arrival of the first child, we can also expect that parents experience a time of increased stress in their marital relationship when the child reaches puberty. This experience of stress, of course, is manifest in all communications about everyday management and present in all dyadic interactions. Families are not just well-established groups of individuals with a kind of robust and never-changing set of intragroup relationships. On the contrary, families are more or less fragile constructs that have to adapt to challenges generated by individual developmental processes. These challenges imply that established regulations no longer fit when children arrive at higher levels of individual growth. Under individual and family developmental perspectives, children have to widen their horizon by watching their parents tackle new problems, and the parents have to reflect their own roles as functioning models for the child to find new ways to handle controversies and conflicts. Families differ considerably in openness for new solutions, the way they pay attention to each others' needs and the sensitivity to leave enough space for the others' idiosyncrasies.

The different modalities by which parents and children communicate with one another have long been considered as salient mediators for rules, regulations, and values inside the family. Moreover, as knowledge grew about intricate details of the relatedness between mother–child and father–child communication (e.g., Clarke-Stewart, 1988), more concepts emerged carrying a sophisticated view of a family's impact on a child's well-being and the parents' own development (Silverberg, 1996). Even the degree of harmony and the kind of consensus-seeking or dissent-confirming behaviors found in parent–parent discussions and watched by the child are obviously affecting the child's well-being and do show an apparent "spillover" effect (Engfer, 1988) when parent–child interactions are considered. As the meta-analysis of Erel and Burman (1995) has revealed, marital communication is highly influential for a child's acquisition of social skills and the quality of well-being of the entire family.

Clinging to established patterns or leaving space for the exploration of new formats, especially during periods of developmental change, are important factors in families' provision for a child's easy and satisfying or arduous and dissatisfying course of development (Cowan, P. A.,1991). Specific ways of expressing needs and concerns and of conveying anger and satisfaction within the family provide the child with possible tools to be used when developmental changes occur and new formats in relationships are to be negotiated. When parents successfully grant a kind of "secure base" for the child and live a model of consensual and warm exchange in their marital relationship, the child can try out a wider scale of behaviors than can an adolescent from a family where no such emotional base is available and communication between parents is marked by discouraging forms of dissensus and mistrust. Therefore, elements of everyday communication within the family and their application across situations and time must be the target of investigations dealing with the different individual transition processes as these elements, at least in part, constitute the components of a child's kit from which he or she can construct the tools necessary to master individual developmental pathways.

NOTES

[1] For the log-linear model search process BMDP 4 F Program was used.

[2] Main effect models were not interpretable as frequency contours along main effects were either empirically predefined (unequal frequencies of time periods or cluster groups) or trivial (unequal frequencies across categories' different levels).

[3] In order to compute parameter estimates, contrasts were formed by using one of the categories as anchor category or reference, against which the others were compared. For the time comparison, the fourth wave (t4) was taken as the reference time against which the other three times wave 1 (t1), wave 6 (t6), and wave 8 (t8) were contrasted. For the cluster comparisons, the secure cluster (C3) was chosen as anchor against which both the habitual cluster (C1) and the ambivalent cluster (C2)

were contrasted. Finally, for the selected communication variables "Communication Style," the level "giving attention" (L2) was contrasted against the other three levels "statement" (L1), teaching (L3), and "negotiation" (L4), and the variable "closeness" the level "low" (L2) was chosen as anchor against which the other levels "very low" (L1), "high" (L3) and "very high" (L4) were contrasted. Parameter estimates are given in normalized format as z values. Contrasts for z values are indicated for cluster membership and time only, as contrasts for the category levels are identical in all terms containing [O]. Parameters are estimated according to the predefined contrasts, an estimation for the missing parameter of the anchor category can be assessed by summing the z-values of the entire row up to zero. The same procedure holds for all respective columns or rows of a m x n table.

REFERENCES

Beckwith, L., Cohen, S. E., & Hamilton, C. E. (1995). *Mother-infant interaction and parental divorce predict attachment representation at late adolescence.* Paper presented at the biennial meeting of the Society for Research in Child Development. Indianapolis, IN.

Bell, R. Q. (1968). A reinterpretation of the direction of effects in studies of socialization. *Psychological Review, 75,* 81-95.

Belsky, J. (1981). Early human experience: A family perspective. *Development Psychology, 17,* 3-23.

Belsky, J., Crnic, K., & Gable, S. (1995). The determinants of coparenting in families with toddler boys: Spousal differences and daily hassles. *Child Development, 66,* 629-642.

Bowlby, J. (1969). *Attachment and loss: Vol. I. Attachment.* London: The Hogarth Press.

Bowlby, J. (1973). *Attachment and loss: Vol. II. Separation.* London: The Hogarth Press.

Boyum, L. A., & Parke, R. D. (1995). The role of family emotional expressiveness in the development of children's social competence. *Journal of Marriage and the Family, 57,* 593-608.

Burgess, E. (1926). The family as a unity of interacting personalities. *Family, 7,* 3-9.

Clarke-Stewart, K. A. (1978). And daddy makes three: The father's impact on mother and young child. *Child Development, 49,* 466-478.

Clarke-Stewart, K. A. (1988). Parents' effects on children's development: A decade of progress? *Journal of Applied Developmental Psychology, 9,* 41-84.

Cowan, C. P., & Cowan, P. A. (1987). Men's involvement in parenthood: Identifying the antecedents and understanding the barriers. In P. W. Berman & F. A. Pedersen (Eds.), *Men's transition to parenthood* (pp. 145-174). Hillsdale, NJ: Erlbaum.

Cowan, C. P., & Cowan, P. A. (1992). *When partners become parents: The big life change for couples.* New York: Basic Books.

Cowan, C. P., Cowan, P. A., Heming, G., & Miller, N. B. (1991). Becoming a family: Marriage, parenting, and child development. In P. A. Cowan & M. Hetherington, (Eds.), *Family transitions* (pp. 79-109). Hillsdale, NJ: Erlbaum.

Cowan, P. A. (1991). Individual and family life transitions: A proposal for a new definition. In P. A. Cowan & M. Hetherington (Eds.), *Family transitions* (pp. 3–30). Hillsdale, NJ: Erlbaum.

Cowan, P. A., & Cowan, C. P. (1988). Changes in marriage during the transition to parenthood. In G. Y. Michaels & W. A. Goldberg (Eds.), *The transition to parenthood: Current theory and research* (pp. 114–154). Cambridge, UK: Cambridge University Press.

Cummings, E. M., & Davies, P. (1994). *Children and marital conflict: The impact of family dispute and resolution.* New York: Guilford.

Cummings, J. S., Pellegrini, D. S., Notarius, C. I., & Cummings, E. M. (1989). Children's responses to angry adult behavior as a function of marital distress and history of interparental hostility. *Child Development, 60,* 1035–1043.

Davies, P. T., Myers, R. L., & Cummings, E. M. (1996). Responses of children and adolescents to marital conflict scenarios as a function of the emotionality of conflict endings. *Merrill-Palmer Quarterly, 42,* 1–21.

Dunn, J. (1988). *The beginnings of social understanding.* Cambridge, MA: Harvard University Press.

Duvall, E. (1977). *Marriage and family development.* New York: Lippincott.

Emery, R. E. (1982). Interparental conflict and the children of discord and divorce. *Psychological Bulletin, 92,* 310–330.

Engfer, A. (1988). The interrelatedness of marriage and the mother–child relationship. In R. A. Hinde & J. S. Hinde (Eds.), *Relationships within families: Mutual influences* (pp. 104–118). Oxford, UK: Oxford University Press.

Erel, O., & Burman, B. (1995). Interrelatedness of marital and parent–child relations: A meta-analytic review. *Psychological Bulletin, 118,* 108–132.

Escalona, S. K. (1973). Basic modes of social interaction: Their emergence and pattering during the first two years of life. *Merrill Palmer Quarterly, 19,* 205-232.

Evers, M., & Namboodiri, N. K. (1978). On the design matrix strategy in the analysis of categorical data. In K. F. Schuessler (Ed.), *Sociological methodology* (pp. 86–111). San Francisco: Jossey Bass.

Feldman, S. S., Fisher, L., & Seitel, L. (1997). The effect of parents' marital satisfaction on young adults' adaptation: A longitudinal study. *Journal of Research on Adolescence, 7,* 55–80.

Fienberg, S. E. (1980). *The analysis of cross-classified categorical data.* Cambridge, MA: MIT Press.

George, C., Kaplan, N., & Main, M. (1984). *Attachment interview for adults.* Unpublished manuscript, University of California, Berkeley, CA.

Gottman, J. M., & Katz, L. (1989). Effect of marital discord on young children's peer interaction and health. *Developmental Psychology, 25,* 373–381.

Grotevant, H. D, & Cooper, C. R. (1986). Individuation in family relationships. *Human Development, 29,* 82–100.

Hamilton, C. E. (1994). *Continuity and discontinuity of attachment from infancy through adolescence.* Unpublished doctoral dissertation, University of California, Los Angeles.

Hauser, S. T., Powers, S. I., & Noam, G. G. (1991). *Adolescents and their families.* New York: The Free Press.

Havighurst, R. J. (1953). *Human development and education*. New York: David McKay.

Hill, J. P. (1987). Research on adolescents and their families: Past and prospect. In W. Damon (Ed.), *New directions for child development: Adolescent health and social behavior* (Vol. 37, pp. 13–32). San Francisco, CA: Jossey-Bass.

Katz, L. F., & Gottman, J. M. (1993). Patterns of marital conflict predict children's internalizing and externalizing behaviors. *Developmental Psychology, 29*, 940–950.

Keppler, A. (1994). *Tischgespraeche. Ueber Formen kommunikativer Vergemeinschaftung am Beispiel der Konversation in Familien* [Dinner talk. Family conversations as an example of form of communicative sozialization]. Frankfurt: Suhrkamp.

Kreppner, K. (1995). Differential experiences within the family during adolescence: Consistencies of relationship assessments and concrete communication behaviors over time. In J. J. Hox, B. F. van der Meulen, J. M. A. Janssens, J. J. F. ter Laak, & L. W. C. Tavecchio (Eds.), *Advances in family research* (pp. 103–122). Amsterdam: Thesis Publishers.

Kreppner, K. (1996). Kommunikationsverhalten zwischen Eltern und ihren jugendlichen Kindern und der Zusammenhang mit Indikatoren des Selbstwertgefuehls [Self-esteem and verbal behavior in interactions of parents and adolescents]. *Praxis der Kinderpsychologie und Kinderpsychiatrie, 45*, 130–147.

Kreppner, K., & Ullrich, M. (1996). Familien-Codier-System. Beschreibung eines Codiersystems zur Beurteilung von Kommunikationsverhalten in Familiendyaden [Family Coding System. Description of a coding system for communicative behavior in family dyads]. *Materialien aus der Bildungsforschung, 57*, Berlin: Max-Planck Institute.

Kreppner, K., & Ullrich, M. (1997, April). *The quality of parent–parent communication in the family and its impact on adolescent development*. Paper presented at the Biennial Meeting of the Society for Research in Child Development, Washington, DC.

Lamb, M. (1975). Father: Forgotten contributors to child development. *Human Development, 18*, 245–266.

Lewis, M., & Feiring, C. (1978). The child's social world. In R. M. Lerner & G. B. Spanier (Eds.), *Child influences on marital and family interaction* (pp. 47–69). New York: Academic Press.

Mayseless, O. (1996). Attachment pattern and their outcomes. *Human Development, 39*, 206–233.

McHale, J. P. (1995). Coparenting and triadic interactions during infancy: The roles of marital distress and child gender. *Developmental Psychology, 31*, 985–996.

Olson, D. H., & McCubbin, H. I. (1983). *Families*. London: Sage.

Parke, R. D. (1979). Perspectives on father–infant interaction. In J. D. Osofsky (Ed.), *Handbook of infant development* (pp. 549–590). New York: Wiley.

Parke, R. D., & Buriel, R. (in press). Socialization in the family: Ethnic and ecological perspectives. In N. Eisenberg (Ed.), *Mussen's Handbook of Child Psychology*. New York: Wiley.

Pedersen, F. A. (1975). *Mother, father, and infant as an interaction system*. Paper presented at the Annual Convention of the American Psychological Association, Chicago.

Pedersen, F. A., Anderson, B. J., & Cain, R. L. (1980). Parent–infant and husband–wife interactions observed at age five months. In F. A. Pedersen (Ed.), *The father–infant relationship* (pp. 71–86). New York: Praeger.

Pedersen, F. A., Yarrow, L., Anderson, B., & Cain, R. (1978). Conceptualization of father influences in the infancy period. In M. Lewis & L. Rosenblum (Eds.), *The social network of the developing infant* (pp. 267–289). New York: Plenum.

Reiss, D. (1981). *The family's construction of reality.* Cambridge, MA: Harvard University Press.

Rheingold, H. L. (1969). The social and socializing infant. In D. A. Goslin (Ed.), *Handbook of socialization theory and research* (pp. 779–790). Chicago: Rand McNally.

Rindskopf, D. (1990). Nonstandard log-linear models. *Psychological Bulletin, 108,* 150–162.

Robin, A., & Weiss, J. (1980). Criterion related validity of behavioral and self-report measures of problem-solving communication skills in distressed and non-distressed parent–adolescent dyads. *Behavioral Assessment, 2,* 339–352.

Shifflett-Simpson K., & Cummings E. M. (1996). Mixed message resolution and children's response to interadult conflict. *Child Development, 67,* 437–448.

Silverberg, S. B. (1996). Parents' well-being at their children's transition to adolescence. In C. D. Ryff & M. M. Seltzer (Eds.), *The parental experience in midlife* (pp. 215–254). Chicago: University of Chicago Press.

Silverberg, S. B., & Steinberg, L. (1990). Psychological well-being of parents with early adolescent children. *Developmental Psychology, 26,* 658–666.

Spiel, C., Kreppner, K., & Von Eye, A. (1995). Die Familien-Beziehungs-Skalen, FBS: Bericht ueber die Entwicklung eines Screening Instruments zur Erfassung von Beziehung Jugendlicher zu ihren Eltern [Family Relations Scales. Report on the development of a screening instrument for the assessment of adolescents–parent relations]. *Diagnostica, 41,* 322–333.

Steele, H., Steele, M., & Fonagy, P. (1996). Associations among attachment classifications of mothers, fathers, and their infants. *Child Development, 67,* 541–555.

Van Ijzendoorn, M. H. (1996). Commentary (in response to Mayseless, O. 1996. Attachment patterns and their outcomes, Human Development, 39, 206–223). *Human Development, 39,* 224–231.

Von Eye, A., Kreppner, K., & Wessels, H. (1992). Differential change in systems of categorical variables. In J. B. Asendorpf & J. Valsiner (Eds.), *Stability and change in development: A study of methodological reasoning* (pp. 21–53). Newbury Park, CA: Sage.

Von Eye, A., Kreppner, K., & Wessels, H. (1994). Log-linear modeling of categorical data in developmental research. In D. L. Featherman, R. M. Lerner, & M. Perlmutter (Eds.), *Life-span development and behavior* (Vol. 12, pp. 225–248). Hillsdale, NJ: Erlbaum.

Ward, J. H. (1963). Hierarchical grouping to optimize an objective function. *Journal of the American Statistical Association, 58,* 236–244.

Waters, E., Merrick, S. K., Albersheim, L. J., & Treboux, D. (1995, April). *Attachment security from infancy to early adulthood: A 20-year longitudinal study.* Paper presented at the biennal meeting of the Society for Research in Child Development, Indianapolis, IN.

Watzlawick, P., Beavin, J. H., & Jackson, D. D. (1967). *Pragmatics of human communication*. New York: Norton.

Wickens, T. D. (1989). *Multiway contingency tables analysis for the social sciences*. Hillsdale, NJ: Erlbaum.

Youniss, J. (1983). Social construction of adolescence by adolescents and parents. In H. D. Grotevant & C. R. Cooper (Eds.), *Adolescent development in the family: New directions for child development* (pp. 93–110). San Francisco: Jossey Bass.

Youniss, J. (1989). Parent–adolescent relationships. In W. Damon (Ed.), *Child development today and tomorrow* (pp. 379–392). San Francisco: Jossey Bass.

Youniss, J. & Smollar, J. (1985). *Adolescent relations with mothers, fathers, and friends*. Chicago: University of Chicago Press.

Zimmermann, P. (1994). *Bindung im Jugendalter: Entwicklung und Umgang mit aktuellen Anforderungen* [Attachment in adolescence: Development and interaction with present circumstances]. Doctoral dissertation, University of Regensburg.

Chapter 7

Family Interaction as a Context for The Development of Adolescent Autonomy*

Marc Noom
Utrecht University

Maja Deković
Utrecht University

Parent–adolescent relations are transformed during adolescence from patterns in which adults are in authority to patterns of mutuality (e.g., Grotevant & Cooper, 1986; Steinberg, 1990; Youniss, 1983). Both adolescents and parents face the task of changing their relationship in ways that reflect the increasing symmetry in their contributions to it. Adolescents must gain autonomy from the thoughts, feelings, and actions of their parents. They experience an increasing desire to make their own choices and to act accordingly. Parents, on the other hand, need to adapt to adolescents' desire for autonomy by creating an opportunity for them to experiment with their new role and by encouraging them to do so.

This study seeks to examine the relationship between parental behavior and adolescent autonomy in more detail through observation of family interactions. We first describe adolescents' task of developing autonomy, and then present a theoretical overview of the parental task of stimulating their development. Next, we present a coding system designed to explicate the

* This research was supported by a grant from the Dutch Ministry of Health and Culture (PCOJ).

relationship between parent stimulation and the development of adolescent autonomy and present findings based on this coding scheme.

AUTONOMY

Adolescents must successfully master several developmental tasks before they can achieve healthy psycho-social functioning as an adult. One element of this transition is the development of *autonomy* (Havighurst, 1948). Examination of the literature suggests that autonomy has been operationalized differently by a variety of researchers, and that results vary by the definition used (e.g., Bekker, 1991; Dworkin, 1988; Koestner & Losier, 1996; Lamborn & Steinberg, 1993; Metaal, 1992; Ryan, 1991, 1993; Ryan & Lynch, 1989; Silverberg & Gondoli, 1996; Steinberg & Silverberg, 1986). The central idea that underlies the concept of autonomy, however, is indicated by the etymology of the term: *autos* (self) and *nomos* (rule), which can be translated into the ability to regulate one's own life. However, the wide variety of conceptualizations indicates that "autonomy is probably more appropriately conceptualized as a chapter heading, under which a variety of putatively related phenomena might be grouped, than as a unidimensional aspect of adolescent psychosocial development" (Steinberg & Silverberg, 1986, p. 841). We utilize an integrative model and conceptualize autonomy as a set of abilities that emerges during adolescence (Noom, 1997). Each ability is a separate developmental task necessary for the self-regulation of behavior. Empirical analyses confirmed the convergent and divergent validity of three dimensions of autonomy (Noom, Deković, & Meeus, 1997): (1) attitudinal autonomy; (2) emotional autonomy; and (3) functional autonomy.

Attitudinal autonomy concerns the perception adolescents have about their goals, wishes, desires, preferences, and values. As adolescents' cognitive abilities develop, they become increasingly able to consider multiple possibilities and decide which option to choose. This ability is a prerequisite to self-regulation of behavior. *Emotional autonomy* is an affective process and involves the perception of independence from parents and peers, while also maintaining a positive relationship with them. Both parents and peers make demands on the adolescent when attempting to exert their influence on the adolescent's decisions. Emotional autonomy involves the ability to define one's goals without subordinating personal goals to the wishes of significant others. *Functional autonomy* refers to the ability to develop strategies that allow individuals to achieve their personal goals. This ability incorporates the regulatory process of choosing a strategy and conducting this plan of action.

PARENTAL BEHAVIOR AND ADOLESCENT AUTONOMY

These developmental changes on the part of adolescents require a corresponding change in behavior on the part of parents. The adolescents' ability to deal with these tasks is, at least in part, dependent on the context in which they grow up. Noller (1995) described three ways that the family may promote the competence and confidence with which young people face the transition from childhood to adulthood. First, the family can provide a *model* for adolescents to learn appropriate patterns of communication. In families where parents themselves demonstrate effective communication skills, adolescents are more likely to acquire those skills by observing and imitating their parents. Parents who clearly articulate their opinions about what they think and give reasons for their opinions may stimulate adolescents to think about their own ideas.

Second, the family can reassure the adolescent by creating a *supportive* environment. A warm and affectionate parent–adolescent relationship provides an opportunity for adolescents to explore and express their ideas freely and to test them in a family context without fear of criticism and rejection. Affectionate and supportive parents tend to show respect for the views of their children and are open and responsive to those views. This helps adolescents to achieve a sense of independence, feel free to adopt their own opinions and attitudes, make their own plans, and formulate their own goals. On the other hand, when family interactions are characterized by a great amount of hostility and criticism, adolescents are less likely to be self-confident and more likely to use external standards, rather than their own judgment, as a guide for their behavior. Adolescents growing up in such families tend to be more susceptible to both parental and peer pressures, and less likely to function autonomously.

Finally, parents may enhance adolescent autonomy by *stimulating* adolescents to participate in making important decisions. Parents can motivate their sons and daughters to think about their own ideas and contemplate possible solutions by asking questions and making suggestions. Thus, the renegotiation of roles, rules, and relationships allows adolescents to see their own responsibility in giving direction to their lives.

Empirical studies on the relationship between parenting and adolescent development have primarily confirmed the importance of support and stimulation for facilitating the achievement of independence and becoming an autonomous individual during adolescence (e.g., Fletcher, Darling, Steinberg, & Dornbusch, 1995; Fuhrman & Holmbeck, 1995; Gecas & Seff, 1990; Steinberg, Elmen, & Mounts, 1989; Steinberg, Lamborn, Dornbusch, & Darling, 1992; for a review, see Baumrind, 1991). These studies found a significant relationship between adolescent autonomy and authoritative parenting styles in which parents were highly responsive and demanding (Maccoby & Martin, 1983).

However, these studies have two important disadvantages. Authoritative parenting is conceptualized as a very broad construct which includes many different aspects of parental behavior. This complicates the determination of the specific elements of parenting which are especially beneficial for the development of adolescent autonomy. Furthermore, most of these studies have used adolescents as the only source of information for both individual development and parental practices. This may have unjustly strengthened the hypothesized relationship.

Observational studies of family interaction may provide more objective data on the parent–adolescent relationship. In these studies information is gathered by observing parents and adolescents and by coding their verbal interactions. Thus, observational data eliminate the problem of obtaining both dependent and independent variables from one source.

Several observational studies have focused on the changes in the parent–adolescent relationship and its impact on various aspects of the adolescent's psycho-social development, such as identity (e.g., Cooper, Grotevant, & Condon, 1983; Grotevant & Cooper, 1985), ego-development (e.g., Allen, Hauser, Bell, & O'Connor, 1994; Hauser, Powers, Noam, Jacobson, Weiss, & Follansbee, 1984), depression (e.g., Dadds, Sanders, Morrison, & Rebgetz, 1992), communication (e.g., Vuchinich & Angelelli, 1995), and self-esteem (e.g., Allen, Hauser, Bell, & O'Connor, 1994). However, only a few observational studies have explored the relationship between family interaction and autonomy. Hakim-Larson and Hobart (1987), for example, examined how maternal regulation and daughters' striving for autonomy are reflected in dyadic communication. Their study demonstrated that one aspect of parental regulation—asking questions—enhances the development of adolescent autonomy.

While observational studies have clear advantages over survey methods, they have not yet portrayed the full picture of the relationship between family interaction and adolescent autonomy. Furthermore, the existing coding systems do not seem appropriate for our theoretical perspective on the parent–adolescent relationship. Therefore, the aims of the present study were two-fold. Our primary goal was to perform a detailed analysis on the importance of family interaction as a context for the development of adolescent autonomy. However, to do so, we first needed to develop a coding system that was both suitable for a microanalytical level of analysis and appropriate for the assessment of modeling, supportive, and stimulating parental behavior.

THE CONVERSATION CODING SYSTEM

We developed the Conversation Coding System (Version A, CCS[a], Noom & Deković, 1997) to assist in categorizing the specific aspects of parent–adolescent communication described below. This system was based on the work of Grotevant and Carlson (1987), who distinguished five types of constructs in coding systems for observed interactions: (1) *cognitive constructs*, which refer to patterns of interaction that provide information to family members; (2) *affective constructs*, which express emotions toward family members; (3) *interpersonal process regulators*, which regulate the interaction within the family; (4) *structural constructs*, which reflect patterns of relationship within the family; and (5) *dominance constructs*, referring to control, sanctions, or conflict within the family. We incorporated these five types of constructs into the CCS[a], in order to cover the full range of communication behavior. These five constructs were combined into three dimensions for the CCS[a] (see Table 1).

The *functional* dimension is a combination of cognitive, affective, and regulatory constructs. *Cognitive* constructs refer to giving an opinion and providing information. Examples are simple agreements ("Yes"), founded agreements ("Yes, because ..."), explanations ("I think that because ..."), factual information ("She is 21"), doubts ("Well, I don't know"), simple disagreements ("No"), and founded disagreements ("No, because ..."). *Affective* constructs in the form of emotional expressions are responsiveness ("What is your opinion about this?"), encouragements ("Don't worry, we'll solve this"), positive humor ("Let's fly to the moon!"), statements of feelings ("I am very angry!"), negative humor ("I love these endless discussions"), defensiveness ("But she started it!"), and criticism ("You are stupid!"). *Regulatory* constructs reflect the aim of regulating the situation, and consist of suggestions ("Let's do ..."), questions ("What do you mean by that?"), accepting responsibility ("We have to solve this problem"), conclusions ("I conclude that ..."), denying responsibility ("I don't care"), refusals ("I don't want to do this"), and commands ("I want you to ...").

The *structural* dimension refers to whether the attitude of the speaker is compliant or opposing toward the other person. These structural constructs give an indication of the general pattern of family interaction. Finally, the *dominance* dimension refers to whether the utterance can be regarded as an initiative or a response. These dominance constructs reflect the tendency of a speaker either to play an active part in the discussion or to be a more passive participant in the conversation.

Adopting Noller's (1995) view that family interaction is most beneficial for the development of adolescent autonomy when it is characterized by a high degree of modeling, support, and stimulation, we propose several hypotheses. The modeling hypothesis implies that parental behavior in the form of expressing and founding an opinion enhances autonomy by functioning as a role model. The support hypothesis indicates that parents providing support through responsiveness, warmth, and affection increase their child's autonomy by creating a supportive environment. The stimula-

TABLE 1.   Dimensions and Codes of the Conversation Coding System (CCSᵃ)

Dimension	Code	Description	
		STRUCTURAL DIMENSION	
		Structural Constructs	
		(being compliant [+] or opposing [−])	
FUNCTIONAL DIMENSION			
Cognitive Constructs	FA.	Founded Agreement	+
(giving information)	SA.	Simple Agreement	+
	EX.	Explanation	+
	FI.	Factual Information	+/−
	DO.	Doubt	−
	SD.	Simple Disagreement	−
	FD.	Founded Disagreement	−
Affective Constructs	RS.	Responsiveness	+
(expressing an emotion)	EN.	Encouragement	+
	PH.	Positive Humor	+
	SF.	Statement of Feelings	+/−
	NH.	Negative Humor	−
	DF.	Defensiveness	−
	CR.	Criticism	−
Regulatory Constructs	SG.	Suggestion	+
(directing the discussion)	QU.	Question	+
	AR.	Accepting Responsibility	+
	CN.	Conclusion	+/−
	DR.	Denying Responsibility	−
	RF.	Refusal	−
	CM.	Command	−
DOMINANCE DIMENSION			
Dominance Constructs	..I	Initiative	
(being active or reactive)	..R	Response	
OTHER	PA	Paraphrase	
	IC	Irrelevant Comment	
	UU	Uncodeable Utterance	
	MP	Minimal Positive Utterance	
	MN	Minimal Negative Utterance	

tion hypothesis suggests that parents can encourage autonomy by regulatory acts such as asking questions and making suggestions. Thus, we hypothesize that family interaction which is most beneficial for the adolescent's development of autonomy is characterized by a high degree of modeling, support, and stimulation. This pattern of interaction seems to correspond closely to the adolescent's need for a balance between individuality (i.e., the drive for independence and self-assertion) and connectedness (i.e., the need to be included and committed; Baumrind, 1991).

METHOD

Subjects

The subjects in this study were members of 40, two-parent families from a wide range of socioeconomic and educational backgrounds. The families were drawn from a larger sample of 508 families who participated in a national survey "Child Rearing in The Netherlands in the 1990s" (Rispens, Hermanns, & Meeus, 1996). Each family included an adolescent between 12 and 18 years old; 23 families had a son, and 17 families had a daughter. The mean age of adolescents was 14.35, and all parents were born in The Netherlands.

Procedure

The observation session usually took place during the early evening when the target adolescent, mother, and father were present. As we wanted to capture both conflictual and cooperative aspects of family interaction, two tasks were chosen. In Planning a Vacation Together, the family makes plans for a fictional 3-week vacation for which they have unlimited funds (Grotevant & Cooper, 1985). The family members are asked to plan a day-to-day schedule and to write down the location and activities planned for each day. This task was designed to elicit active participation from all family members and to provide an opportunity for the adolescent's interest and expertise to contribute to the family's decisions.

A Revealed Differences Task was chosen to stimulate conflict. The family members were asked to discuss a specific emotionally charged family problem and come to a consensus regarding the solution of the problem. At the beginning of the session, each individual completed the Issues Checklist (Prinz, Foster, Kent, & O'Leary, 1979; Robin & Foster, 1984) to identify issues of concern that led to disagreements within the family. The respondents were asked if 44 specific issues (e.g., chores, curfew, clothing, homework, etc.) took place during the previous four weeks. If an issue had been discussed, they were asked to indicate the frequency and rate the intensity of the discussions. The observer then selected three topics which all family members had specified, and which produced the most negative affect. The family members were asked to discuss these topics, one by one, and to find a solution for each topic.

Each task lasted 10 minutes. The audiotaped discussions were transcribed verbatim indicating the source and object of each utterance. Transcripts preserved pauses, interruptions, and nonverbal cues such as laughter and hesitation. To minimize inference by coders, the observer's remarks were also included (e.g., joke, mockery, etc.).

Measures

In observing *family interaction,* each utterance contained in the transcription was given two codes: one code for the functional dimension, referring to the cognitive, affective, or regulatory function, which simultaneously implied a structural code for the positive or negative nature of the utterance; and a second code for the dominance dimension, referring to the utterance as an initiative or a response. Two raters coded the transcripts after an 83% agreement was reached in a training procedure. The measurement consisted of the total number of utterances each family member had in each coding category.

Adolescent autonomy was measured by a 15-item questionnaire (Noom, 1997) consisting of three, 5-item scales. Each scale measured one of the aspects of autonomy described earlier: (1) the ability to see what your possibilities are and to choose among them (e.g., "When asked, I know what I want"); (2) the ability to resist emotional pressure from parents and peers (e.g., "When I disagree with somebody, I express this"); and (3) the ability to carry out a plan to achieve a specific goal (e.g., "I always go for a goal"). Adolescents were asked to respond on a 5-point scale (1 = completely disagree to 5 = completely agree). The internal consistencies of the three scales were .70 for the ability to choose, .61 for emotional independence, and .64 for the ability to exercise control. Scale scores were computed by averaging the responses to the items on each scale.

RESULTS

Descriptive Statistics of the Communication Variables

Table 2 presents the means and standard deviations of the 27 interaction codes. The table shows a great diversity in the means and standard deviations, reflecting a considerable variety in the frequency of aspects of speech. The most frequently used utterances were simple agreements, explanations and suggestions, indicating a relatively pleasant family climate overall.

Multivariate analyses of variances (MANOVA) for each code with families as subjects, and family-membership as a within-subject factor, indicate that adolescents showed more simple agreements, simple disagreements, and more defensiveness than their parents (see Table 2). Furthermore, adolescents provided fewer explanations, factual information, responsiveness, encouragement, questions, acceptance of responsibility, conclusions, commands, and initiatives than their parents. Fathers expressed less doubt, founded disagreements, and feelings than their wives and children. Mothers gave more suggestions than their husbands and children.

TABLE 2. Means, standard deviations and ranges of the family-interaction codes

Codes	Child		Mother		Father		F-value
	M	SD	M	SD	M	SD	
FUNCTIONAL DIMENSION							
Cognitive Constructs							
Founded Agreement	1.4	1.6	1.3	1.4	.9	1.2	1.66
Simple Agreement	31.5[a]	17.0	24.1[b]	15.5	20.3[b]	10.8	9.29*
Explanation	17.6[a]	13.7	26.7[b]	13.3	24.3[b]	12.8	8.01*
Factual Information	6.2[a]	11.0	9.9[b]	5.9	10.0[b]	7.6	3.66*
Doubt	1.9[a]	2.3	1.4[a]	1.8	.7[b]	1.2	5.93*
Simple Disagreement	10.3[a]	7.9	5.8[b]	4.2	6.4[b]	6.1	9.98*
Founded Disagreement	5.0[a]	5.1	4.8[a]	3.9	2.9[b]	2.5	5.06*
Affective Constructs							
Responsiveness	.9[a]	1.7	6.5[b]	5.3	4.5[c]	4.6	20.90*
Encouragement	.2[a]	.6	1.0[b]	1.4	.8[b]	.9	7.97*
Positive Humor	2.9	4.6	2.9	3.2	2.5	2.4	2.41
Statement of Feelings	1.0[a]	1.4	.8[a]	.9	.4[b]	.6	3.99*
Negative Humor	.5	1.5	.3	.5	.9	2.3	1.60
Defensiveness	4.9[a]	5.3	.2[b]	.4	.7[b]	2.6	28.00*
Criticism	4.3	4.3	5.0	4.7	4.8	4.0	.35
Regulatory Constructs							
Suggestion	14.9[a]	9.0	18.9[b]	9.4	17.1[a]	7.5	3.37*
Question	8.5[a]	6.9	17.1[b]	13.4	17.4[b]	12.7	8.47*
Accepting Responsibility	.3[a]	.6	1.5[b]	1.6	1.4[b]	1.4	9.78*
Conclusion	1.9[a]	2.4	4.5[b]	4.3	5.6[b]	5.2	8.66*
Denying Responsibility	.1	.4	.1	.2	.1	.3	.53
Refusal	.1	.2	.1	.2	.0	.0 -	
Command	.9[a]	1.7	2.9[b]	2.8	2.9[b]	2.9	10.50*
DOMINANCE DIMENSION							
Initiatives	101.5[a]	46.2	136.5[b]	51.6	124.6[b]	43.2	7.63*
OTHER							
Paraphrase	1.4	2.5	2.5	2.9	1.7	2.3	2.14
Irrelevant Comment	.0	.0	.1	.4	.1	.5	-
Uncodeable Utterance	5.9	4.9	5.8	4.8	6.4	3.6	.43
Minimal Positive	9.8[a]	7.7	8.4[a]	6.7	4.3[b]	4.2	11.93*
Minimal Negative	3.2[a]	3.3	1.0[b]	1.0	1.6[b]	3.0	10.62*
TOTAL							
Number of Utterances	134.9	53.9	153.0	55.0	138.6	47.6	1.96

Note. Means with different superscripts differ significantly at $p < .01$.

Transformation of Communication Variables

As considerable differences were found between individuals in the total number of verbalizations produced during interaction, we considered two alternate approaches to the use of raw frequencies. First, proportional scores were computed by dividing the frequencies of the communication variables by the number of total utterances for each person. The correlations between proportional scores and scores for the raw variables ranged from .54 to .97, indicating a great variety in the difference between the raw frequencies and the proportional scores. Hence, proportional scores were not used because the correspondence between the raw scores and the proportional scores was too low.

Second, a square root transformation was applied to the communication variables to adjust for the positive skewness of the communication variables. As skewness can unjustly strengthen or weaken a relationship, transformation of the distribution is recommended (Stevens, 1986). The correlations between the transformed and raw scores ranged from .88 to .99, which indicates a high level of correspondence between the two scores. Thus, the transformed scores were used to complete the analyses.

Due to the low frequencies of some variables, new variables were computed by combining the scores of the following conceptually similar categories: simple and founded agreements; simple and founded disagreements and doubts; encouragements and responsiveness; defensiveness, and criticism. As the frequencies for refusal and denial of responsibility were extremely low, they were dropped from the analyses.

Factor Analyses of the Communication Variables

Separate factor analyses were conducted for the aggregated cognitive, affective, and regulatory constructs to examine the structure of these domains (see Table 3). For the cognitive constructs, two factors emerged for all participants. For mothers and adolescents, the first factor included explanations and disagreements, referring to an opposing interaction-style of *arguing*. The second factor included factual information and agreements, which can be described as a more compliant style of *accommodating*. The verbal behavior of the father, on the other hand, followed a different pattern. Instead of either arguing or accommodating, fathers appeared to interact with the other family members by sometimes agreeing or disagreeing, and sometimes explaining or providing factual information.

Regarding the affective constructs, there was a clear opposing or *antipathetic* style for adolescents and both parents, consisting of negative humor and criticism. In addition, there was a compliant or *sympathetic* pattern of the affective constructs consisting of positive humor and responsiveness.

TABLE 3. Factor structure and loadings of cognitive, affective, and regulatory communication variables

Child		Mother		Father	
Cognitive Constructs					
I Explanation	.91	Explanation	.79	Explanation	.66
Disagreement	.90	Disagreement	.86	Disagreement	.62
				Factual Information	.71
				Agreement	.72
II Factual Information	.79	Factual Information	.89		
Agreement	.79	Agreement	.62		
Affective Constructs					
I Negative Humor	.71	Negative Humor	.56	Negative Humor	.90
Criticism	.78	Criticism	.92	Criticism	.91
II Positive Humor	.88	Positive Humor	.77	Positive Humor	.79
Responsiveness	.65	Responsiveness	.60	Responsiveness	.78
Regulatory Constructs					
I Suggestion	.57	Suggestion	.73	Suggestion	.73
Question	.69	Question	.76	Question	.75
Conclusion	.75	Conclusion	.79	Conclusion	.69
Command	.67				
II		Command	.98	Command	.95

The regulatory constructs also revealed a different picture for adolescents and parents. For both parents a compliant or *negotiating* style emerged in the form of suggestions, questions, and conclusions. A second factor consisted of imposing commands and was labeled an *imposing* style. For adolescents, however, a single factor emerged and these two ways of regulating the conversation were integrated.

Relationship Between Family Interaction and Autonomy

The relationship between family interaction and the development of adolescent autonomy was examined through correlational analyses. We tested the hypothesis that compliant aspects of parental behavior provide the best context for the development of adolescents' autonomy by computing the correlations between the accommodating, empathetic, and negotiating style of the parents on one hand and the attitudinal, emotional, and functional autonomy of adolescents on the other hand. A significant relationship was found between an accommodating interaction style and attitudinal autonomy for mothers ($r = .38$). In other words, expressing agreements and providing information by the mother is related to a greater confidence of adolescents in their own ideas. A nonsignificant trend was found between the sympathetic style and attitudinal autonomy ($r = .24$), meaning that maternal responsiveness and positive humor may also contribute to a greater attitudinal independence. Finally a significant relationship was found between a maternal negotiating style and attitudinal autonomy ($r = .43$). This indicates that offering suggestions, asking questions, and proposing conclusions is also associated with adolescents who have a greater confidence in their own ideas.

For the fathers, a nonsignificant trend indicated that their accommodating behavior might be positively related to attitudinal autonomy ($r = .17$). Contrary to what was expected, we found a negative correlation between sympathetic behavior of the fathers and attitudinal autonomy ($r = -.36$). In other words, responsiveness and positive humor of the father is related to the adolescents' perception of *less* independence with regard to their own ideas. Finally, a significant relationship was found between paternal negotiation and attitudinal autonomy ($r = .28$). This means that suggestions, questions, and conclusions on the part of the father are associated with higher adolescent attitudinal independence.

DISCUSSION

Research on the characteristics of parent–child relationships is often based on individual perceptions of parenting and individual perceptions of psychosocial development. These perceptions of parents and children refer to one's own behavior or the other person's behavior, and therefore these perceptions are often biased by personal experiences. Empirical evidence shows that, especially during adolescence, great differences exist in how parents and children perceive their relationship (Paikoff, 1991). To account for this problem, we performed an observational study in a naturalistic setting. An important characteristic of this method is that the measurement of observed behavior is not subject to perceptual biases of the participants. Additionally, observations of interactions between parents and adolescents take into account the reciprocal nature of the parent–child dyad. Observed interactions are, per definition, determined by both participants, whereas survey research only examines individual perceptions of this relationship. This allows for a more contextualized view of the development of adolescent autonomy in which the level of analysis is the relationship instead of the individual (cf. Grotevant & Carlson, 1987; Grotevant & Cooper, 1985, 1986).

Furthermore, the observation of behavior in a natural setting enables the measurement of more ecologically valid data in comparison with the more hypothetical and abstract approach of questionnaires. The present study demonstrates that the chosen tasks can elicit meaningful behavior for both parents and adolescents. No differences were found in the total amount of verbal utterances between parents and adolescents, which indicates that both felt enough at ease to participate fully in the discussions. Other studies have shown that, during behavioral observations, adolescents in particular tend to feel self-conscious, which makes it more difficult for them to act naturally (e.g., Cooper, Grotevant, & Condon, 1983). It appears that the two tasks used in this study made the adolescents feel comfortable enough to take an equal part in the conversation. In addition, the distribution of the scores indicated that these tasks are sensitive enough to differentiate between families and capture the existing differences in styles of conversation.

Validity of the Conversation Coding System

We developed the Conversation Coding System (CCS[a]), for use in the observation of family conversations. The theoretical basis of the CCS[a] rested on an extensive review of existing family interaction coding systems by Grotevant and Carlson (1987) and theories of autonomy development. The results of the present study demonstrate the empirical value of this tool.

The coding system proved to be a reliable instrument for investigating parental and adolescent behavior in an observational setting. Although some differences between the family members emerged, all codes were appropriate for both adolescent and parental behavior. Differences between adolescents and parents generally referred to their different role in the conversation, which seems to reflect the different positions in the family system. As the results are in line with findings from other studies and theoretical conceptions of adolescent autonomy development, these findings provide further support for the validity of the CCS[a].

Factor-analyses of the CCS[a] provided insight into different patterns of interactions within families, and offered an important illustration of the possible positive and negative conversation styles which exist in family interactions. Moreover, the positive styles provide empirical support for the assumed aspects of parental behavior that are important in the development of the adolescent's competence (Noller, 1995): The accommodating style is the equivalent of parental modeling behavior, the sympathetic style is the counterpart of parental support behavior, and the negotiating style is the parallel of parental stimulation behavior.

Relationship Between Family Interaction and Adolescent Autonomy

We hypothesized that parental modeling, support, and stimulation would be positively related to adolescent autonomy. Two of the three hypotheses were confirmed for the relationship between the mothers and the adolescents' attitudinal autonomy. Maternal modeling and stimulation had a positive impact on the adolescents' independence of ideas. The mothers' information giving and agreement appeared to serve as a model for the adolescents' development of their own ideas. The mothers' suggestions, questions, and conclusions seemed to function as a stimulation of the adolescents' attitudinal autonomy, possibly by enabling them to participate during decision-making. While the support-hypothesis was not confirmed, a nonsignificant trend was found.

The stimulation-hypothesis was confirmed for fathers only. Suggestions, questions, and conclusions of the fathers appeared to function as a stimulation for the adolescents' attitudinal autonomy. Contrary to the support-hypothesis, paternal emotional support was negatively related to attitudinal autonomy. Apparently positive feelings and responsiveness of the father constrained attitudinal autonomy. This may be an indication of the different roles that fathers and mothers play in the psychosocial development of their children (cf. Youniss & Smollar, 1985). Mothers may function as an important provider of certainty and safety, a secure base for adolescent exploratory behavior. On the other hand, fathers may be important as the ones who "push the birds out of the nest." Fathers, who provide too much emotional support, may hamper the swarming out of their offspring.

The relationship between verbal communication and emotional or functional autonomy did not reveal a clear picture. This indicates that the parental behavior elicited in this setting can be related to the development of the adolescents' own ideas, values, and goals (i.e., attitudinal autonomy), but not to the emotional independence from parents and peers (i.e., emotional autonomy), and not to the adolescents' ability to develop strategies for achieving their goals (i.e., functional autonomy). One explanation for this finding may be that the present study contained discussion tasks which are conceptually closer to the development of ideas, values, and goals, than the emotional independence from parents and peers or the ability to devise an adequate strategy.

Noom, Deković, and Meeus (1997) demonstrated that the three aspects of autonomy examined here refer to different domains and that they are positively related. Findings from the present study emphasize, once again, the importance and relevance of distinguishing among these domains when conducting research on the development of adolescent autonomy.

Suggestions for Future Research

While this study provided support for the face and construct validity of the CCS[a], more study is needed to examine its external validity. The hypothesized structure of the communication variables also should be examined in a follow-up study. Furthermore, new tasks must be developed to examine the relationship between parental behavior and emotional and functional autonomy. These tasks should involve a more explicit choice between one's own preferences and the preferences of significant others in order to investigate the tendency to conform to the wishes of others. Second, a more explicit test of the ability to think about available strategies and to develop new strategies should be incorporated in the task. This may improve the picture of the relationship between family interaction as a context for the development of adolescent autonomy.

REFERENCES

Allen, J. P., Hauser, S. T., Bell, K. L., & O'Connor, T. (1994). Longitudinal assessment of autonomy and relatedness in adolescent–family interactions as predictors of adolescent ego development and self-esteem. *Child Development, 65*, 179–194.

Baumrind, D. (1991). Parenting styles and adolescent development. In R. M. Lerner, A. C. Petersen, & J. Brooks-Gunn (Eds.), *Encyclopedia of adolescence* (pp. 746–758). New York: Garland.

Bekker, M. H. J. (1991). *De bewegelijke grenzen van het vrouwelijk ego* [The movable boundaries of the female ego]. Delft: Eburon.

Cooper, C. R., Grotevant, H. D., & Condon, S. M. (1983). Individuality and connectedness in the family as a context for adolescent identity formation and role-taking skill. In H. D. Grotevant & C. R. Cooper (Eds.), *Adolescent development in the family: New directions for child development* (pp. 43–58). San Francisco, CA: Jossey-Bass.

Dadds, M. R., Sanders, M. R., Morrison, M., & Rebgetz, M. (1992). Childhood depression and conduct disorder: II. An analysis of family interaction patterns in the home. *Journal of Abnormal Psychology, 101*, 505–513.

Dworkin, G. (1988). *The theory and practice of autonomy*. Cambridge: Cambridge University Press.

Fletcher, A. C., Darling, N. E., Steinberg, L., & Dornbusch, S. (1995). The company they keep: Relation of adolescents' adjustment and behavior to their friends' perceptions of authoritative parenting in the social network. *Developmental Psychology, 31*, 300–310.

Fuhrman, T., & Holmbeck, G. N. (1995). A contextual-moderator analysis of emotional autonomy and adjustment in adolescence. *Child Development, 66*, 793–811.

Gecas, V., & Seff, M. A. (1990). Families and adolescents: A review of the 1980's. *Journal of Marriage and the Family, 52*, 941–958.

Grotevant, H. D. & Carlson, C. I. (1987). Family interaction coding systems: A descriptive review. *Family Process, 26*, 49–74.

Grotevant, H. D., & Cooper, C. R. (1985). Patterns of interaction in family relationships and the development of identity exploration in adolescence. *Child Development, 56*, 415–428.

Grotevant, H. D. & Cooper, C. R. (1986). Individuation in family relationships: A perspective on individual differences in the development of identity and role-taking skill in adolescence. *Human Development, 29*, 82–100.

Hakim-Larson, J., & Hobart, C. J. (1987). Maternal regulation and adolescent autonomy: Mother–daughter resolution of story conflicts. *Journal of Youth and Adolescence, 16,* 153–166.

Havighurst, R. (1948). *Developmental tasks and education.* New York: McKay.

Hauser, S. T., Powers, S. I., Noam, G. G., Jacobson, A. M., Weiss, B., & Follansbee, D. (1984). Familial contexts of adolescent ego development. *Child Development, 55,* 195–213.

Koestner, R., & Losier, G. F. (1996). Distinguishing reactive versus reflective autonomy. *Journal of Personality, 64,* 465–494.

Lamborn, S. D., & Steinberg, L. (1993). Emotional autonomy redux: Revisiting Ryan and Lynch. *Child Development, 64,* 483–499.

Maccoby, E. E., & Martin, J. A. (1983). Socialization in the context of the family: Parent–child interaction. In P. H. Mussen (Ed.), *Handbook of child psychology: Vol 4. Socialization, personality, and social development* (pp. 1–101). New York: Wiley.

Metaal, N. (1992). *Persoonlijke autonomie: Een psychologische studie naar alledaagse verklaringen* [Personal autonomy: A psychological study of ordinary explanations]. Amsterdam: Swets & Zeitlinger.

Noller, P. (1995). Parent–adolescent relationships. In M. A. Fitzpatrick & A. L. Vangelisti (Eds.), *Explaining family interactions* (pp. 77–111). Thousand Oaks, CA: Sage.

Noom, M. J.(1997). *The development of adolescent autonomy: Attitudinal, emotional, and functional autonomy.* Unpublished doctoral dissertation, Utrecht University, The Netherlands.

Noom, M. J., & Deković, M. (1997). *The conversation coding system, version a (CCS^a): A scoring manual.* Unpublished manuscript, Utrecht University, The Netherlands.

Noom, M. J., Deković, M., & Meeus, W. (1997). *Conceptual analysis and measurement of adolescent autonomy: Attitudinal, emotional, and functional autonomy.* Manuscript submitted for publication, Utrecht University, The Netherlands.

Paikoff, R.L. (Ed.). (1991). *Shared views in the family during adolescence.* San Francisco, CA: Jossey-Bass.

Prinz, R. J., Foster, S., Kent, R. N., & O'Leary, K. D. (1979). Multivariate assessment of conflict in distressed and nondistressed mother–adolescent dyads. *Journal of Applied Behavioral Analysis, 12,* 691–700.

Rispens, J., Hermanns, J. & Meeus, W. (1996). *Opvoeden in Nederland* [Child-rearing in The Netherlands]. Assen: Van Gorcum.

Robin, A., & Foster, S. (1984). Problem-solving communication training: A behavioral-family systems approach to parent-adolescent conflict. In P. Karoly & J. Steffen (Eds.), *Adolescent behavior disorders: Foundations and contemporary concerns* (pp. 195–240). Lexington, MA: Lexington Books.

Ryan, R.M. (1991). The nature of the self in autonomy and relatedness. In G. R. Goethals & J. Strauss (Eds.), *Multidisciplinary perspectives on the self* (pp. 208–238). New York: Springer.

Ryan, R. M. (1993). Agency and organization: Intrinsic motivation, autonomy, and the self in psychological development. In J. E. Jacobs (Ed.), *Nebraska symposium on motivation* (Vol. 40, pp. 1–56). Lincoln, NE: University of Nebraska Press.

Ryan, R. M., & Lynch, J. H. (1989). Emotional autonomy versus detachment: Revisiting the vicissitudes of adolescence and young adulthood. *Child Development, 60*, 340–356.

Silverberg, S. B., & Gondoli, D. M. (1996). Autonomy in adolescence: A contextualized perspective. In G. Adams, R. Montemayor, & T. Gullotta (Eds.), *Psychosocial development during adolescence: Progress in developmental contextualism* (pp. 12–61). Thousand Oaks, CA: Sage.

Steinberg, L. (1990). Autonomy, conflict, and harmony in the family relationship. In S. S. Feldman & G. R. Elliott (Eds.), *At the threshold: The developing adolescent* (pp. 255–276). Cambridge, MA: Harvard University Press.

Steinberg, L., Elmen, J. D., & Mounts, N. S. (1989). Authoritative parenting, psychosocial maturity, and academic success among adolescents. *Child Development, 60*, 1424–1436.

Steinberg, L., Lamborn, S. D., Dornbusch, S. M. & Darling, N. (1992). Impact of parenting practices on adolescent achievement: Authoritative parenting, school involvement, and encouragement to succeed. *Child Development, 63*, 1266–1281.

Steinberg, L., & Silverberg, S. B. (1986). The vicissitudes of autonomy in early adolescence. *Child Development, 57*, 841–851.

Stevens, J. (1986). *Applied multivariate statistics for the social sciences*. Hillsdale, NJ: Lawrence Erlbaum.

Vuchinich, S., & Angelelli, J. (1995). Family interaction during problem solving. In M. A. Fitzpatrick & A. L. Vangelisti (Eds.), *Explaining family interactions* (pp.177–205). Thousand Oaks, CA: Sage.

Youniss, J. (1983). Social constructions of adolescence by adolescents and parents. In H. D. Grotevant & C. R. Cooper (Eds.), *Adolescent development in the family: New directions for child development* (pp. 93–109). San Francisco, CA: Jossey-Bass.

Chapter 8

Family Interaction and Psychosocial Adjustment of Adopted and Nonadopted Adolescents

Elke Wild
University of Mannheim

I n most societies, adoption is a widely accepted solution for the care and rearing of children whose biological parents are not able or willing to provide for them. Unfortunately, numerous studies indicate that adopted children are referred for psychological treatment two to five times more frequently than their nonadopted peers, and seem to be especially prone to "internalizing disorders"such as low self-esteem and depression, and to a variety of acting-out problems such as aggression, anti-social behavior, or hyperactivity and learning difficulties (for review, see Brodzinsky, 1990; Klein-Allermann, 1992). The basis of adoptees' vulnerability, however, still remains unclear as few studies have used nonclinical groups of adopted children (Grotevant & McRoy, 1990), and few distinguish between the risk associated with inevitable conditions accompanying adoption, and the risk associated with "hard to place"(e.g., older or physically handicapped children) children (Bohman & Sigvardsson, 1990).

Therefore, the purpose of this chapter is to expand research on adopted adolescents' adjustment by focusing on the impact adoptive family characteristics have on development. As family interactions provide insight into the parent–child relationship and child-rearing patterns, we analyze discourse of adoptive parents and their children to see if interaction patterns are related to adopted adolescents' vulnerability. Theoretically, we refer to self-determination theory (e.g., Ryan, Deci, & Grolnick, 1995) and posit that stressful experiences inherent in adoptive parenthood adversely affect adoptive parents' capability to create a family context that satisfies adoptees' psychological needs and, therefore, promotes optimal development.

This chapter first provides an overview of the central tenets of self-determination theory and outlines the types of stressful experiences adoptive parents face in different stages of the family life cycle. Stressors are examined in terms of their impact on the parent–child relationship and adoptees' adjustment. Next, it presents a study which compares the incidence of maladjustment for adopted and nonadopted adolescents, contrasts adoptive and biological mothers' interaction patterns with their children, and analyzes linkages between maternal interaction patterns and indicators of adopted and nonadopted teenagers' psychosocial adjustment.

SELF-DETERMINATION THEORY

A primary axiom of self-determination theory (e.g., Deci, Eghrari, Patrick, & Leone, 1994; Deci & Ryan, 1994; Ryan et al., 1995) is that people develop through the operation of an organismic integration process, and that many developmental processes occur through the goal-directed, cognitive, and behavioral activities of proactive individuals. Proponents of self-determination theory stress the idea that the *need for competence* and *self-determination*, as well as *the desire for social relatedness* motivate individuals to persist in seeking out stimuli necessary for actualization of their potentials and to engage in activities that are socially valued but that are not necessarily enjoyable. Consequently, the process of organismic integration is assumed to be highly dependent upon *contextual supports* for these three basic psychological needs. Environmental conditions that allow satisfaction of these needs are expected to promote successful internalization and the healthy growth of personality, while environments that frustrate them are thought to impair personal well-being and growth by disrupting integrative tendencies.

Three separate but dynamically related aspects of the family environment are expected to have long-term consequences for the psychological and relational functioning of children (Ryan, 1995; Ryan & Solky, 1996). First, *autonomy support* is present when caregivers abstain from authoritarian discipline techniques and employ support by encouraging self-initiated expression and action, providing the child opportunities to make choices and acknowledging the child's feelings or ideas. Thus, autonomy-supportive parents consider the child's perspective, are responsive to his or her needs, and encourage independent problem-solving. Second, caregivers must provide *structure*, or unambiguous contingencies, a rationale for requests, and meaningful feedback or guidance concerning the child's activity. A structured environment is supposed to facilitate development of self-regulation and self-control. Finally, caregivers must dedicate time, attention, and resources to the child. This caretaker *involvement* includes activities that maintain interpersonal connection, such as practical and emotional support, nurturance, and monitoring.

Proponents of self-determination theory repeatedly have summarized a considerable amount of research indicating, in sum, that self-determination theory has explanatory power with respect to the conditions that promote or undermine optimal functioning (e.g., Deci et al., 1994; Grolnick, Deci, & Ryan, in press; Ryan et al., 1995). Although a great deal of empirical studies has concentrated on teachers' and "normal"parents' styles of supporting children's personal adjustment and school functioning in particular, the implications of this approach to the study of adoptive families are profound. Therefore, we will turn now to reexamining adoption literature from the perspective of self-determination theory. More precisely, we will outline adoption-related problems and experiences that may undermine adoptive parents' involvement as well as their capability to provide guidance or structure and to encourage the child's independent problem-solving and expression of individuality.

ADOPTEES' ADJUSTMENT AND FAMILY CHARACTERISTICS

Adoption research over the past few decades emphasizes several factors that may put adoptees at risk. It is widely accepted that *adverse preplacement experiences*, such as multiple placement disruptions or ongoing foster care may impair adoptees' personal and social development. However, a number of studies indicate that early preplacement experiences explain only a small proportion of variance in adoptees' adjustment (Bohman, 1980; Jungmann, 1987). Furthermore, findings lend support for the argument that negative consequences of early psychological trauma can "fade away"with the opportunity to form new, positive attachments within the adoptive family (Kadushin, 1970). In a similar vein, studies addressing the nature–nurture debate (e.g., Plomin, 1986; Scarr & McCartney, 1983) demonstrate that genetic-based vulnerabilities of adoptees may be suppressed within the warm and supportive adoptive family, and problems may be aggravated when children are placed in a negative environment (for review, see Cadoret, 1990).

Taken together, these results direct the attention to the quality of adoptive family life and to factors that influence adoptive parent's child-rearing behaviors. Proponents of cognitive-developmental theory (e.g., Brodzin-sky, 1990) and social role theory (e.g., Hoffmann-Riem, 1984; Kirk, 1981) have outlined a number of challenges and complications inherent in adoptive parenthood that may impair parents' ability to provide the environment necessary for optimal development.

First, problems may result from *infertility*, as it is the most frequent reason couples decide to adopt a child. Infertile couples are under a great deal of stress for extended periods of time, which may partially explain the linkage between infertility and maladaptive attitudes and behavior patterns of adoptive parents (Knoll & Rehn, 1984; Merz, 1995; Stanton & Dunkel-Schetter, 1991).

Parenting styles may also be influenced by stressful experiences accompanying the *transition* to adoptive parenthood. In contrast to biological parents, adoptive parents are forced to undergo an intensive screening. Moreover, they must cope with the uncertainty of the timing of the adoption process, endure a probationary period following placement, and deal with expressions of misgivings and doubts by friends and relatives. All these experiences may exacerbate a couple's concerns about the child's genetic heritage or their own ability to love the adopted child just as much as a biologically related offspring.

Pre-placement experiences may also adversely affect adoptive parents' efforts in dealing with adoption-related *challenges emerging in later stages of family life cycle*, particularly the task of revealing the adoption to their child. Virtually all adoption specialists agree that, to promote a sense of security, adoptive parents should have frequent discussions that are "in step"with their child's growing understanding of the meaning of adoption (Singer, Brodzinsky, & Braff, 1982). Empirical findings, however, indicate that many adoptive parents feel uncomfortable and anxious about telling the child of his or her adoptive status, overestimate their child's understanding of adoption and, as a result, engage in few discussions of the issue. While parents act in such a defensive way because they want to protect the child from hurtful experiences, this avoidance impairs the establishment of an atmosphere of trust, confidence, and openness which is necessary for the child to feel accepted, cared for, and valued.

Social role theory posits that adoptive families suffer from *role handicaps* such as the lack of role models, rituals, and readily available supports. Although agreement exists that these role handicaps may complicate the construction of a positive and shared view of the nature of adoption and adoptive parenthood, there has been less agreement about the psychological implications of the way family members define the adopted family. Several studies (e.g., Bohman, McRoy, & Grotevant, 1993; Hoffmann-Riem, 1984; Kaye, 1990; Kirk, 1981), however, provide evidence that adoptees' development is optimized in families in which parents acknowledge and accept that the adoptive family situation is different from biological parent-hood. In contrast, problems seem to be more common in families in which parents either deny the differences between adoptive and biological parent-hood or make those inherent differences of adoptive family life the major focus of the family. Rejecting or overemphasizing differences seem to go along with a reduced sense of entitlement to act as the child's full parent, an unfavorable view of the biological parents, discomfort in talking about adoption, a tendency to blame most family problems either on adoption or on the child's biological heritage, and a tendency to convey those bad feel-ings to the child.

Even when we take into account that adoptive families vary in their cop-ing patterns, it seems reasonable to assume that, on average, adoptive par-ents should find it more difficult than biological parents to provide appropriate responses to the child's signals or to establish an accepting and trusting atmosphere in which the child is encouraged to express fantasies and concerns. While these problems are possible throughout childhood, they may be especially prevalent when adoptees enter puberty and—just like their nonadopted agemates—begin to deidealize their parents and strive for individuation (e.g., Youniss & Smollar, 1985). Parents who are un-able to conceive biologically may be more likely to view any disengagement from themselves as abandonment and threat. Moreover, the adoptee's growing interest in his or her roots may shatter a couple's sense of being full-fledged parents and exacerbate feelings of disappointment and uncer-tainty. These feelings, in turn, may reinforce adoptive parents either to re-strict their emotional involvement or hamper the adolescent's emerging sense of individuation by infantilization or suppression of the child's identity-exploration and curiosity about his or her biological roots.

A final source of potential problems is the awareness that there is *no ge-netic connection* between the child and the parents. Theoretically, Grotevant and McRoy (1990) suggest that the vulnerability of adoptees may result, at least in part, from mismatch of parent and child with regard to appearance, personality, intelligence, or attitudes, which leads to impairments in paren-tal sensitivity and responsiveness. Some results (e.g., Schechter & Bertocci, 1990) support this hypothesis and indicate that adoptees perceive the lack of similarities as a significant factor in their sense of frustration, embarrass-ment, and insecurity as an adoptee.

In summary, impairments of adoptive parents' ability to form and sustain a parent–child relationship that is characterized by both autonomy and con-nectedness may result from adoption-related problems such as infertility and stressful experiences accompanying the placement process or later stages of the family life cycle. Their adverse effects on adoptive parents' child-rearing styles and on the adoptees' attachment to parents and their readiness to assimilate the values parents model may cumulate over time.

The developmental tasks of puberty, in particular, may exacerbate problems. At this time, adopted adolescents' growing need to individuate from parental authority and their curiosity about their roots may shatter adoptive parents' sense of being full-fledged parents and exacerbate feelings of disappointment and uncertainty. Given that adoptive parents may react by becoming *either* more controlling *or* less engaged, empathetic, and consistent, it becomes clear why comparisons of adoptive and normal families yielded mixed results. While some researchers found adoptive parents to be more overprotective and insecure as parents, others described them as more demanding with respect to achievement-related issues, having a more asymmetrical (versus reciprocal) relationship to their child, and being oversensitive to their adolescents' strivings for independence (Bohman, 1980; Hoopes, 1982; Sorosky, Baran, & Pannor, 1982; Wild, 1996). From the perspective of self-determination theory, none of these parenting styles reflect the ability or willingness of adoptive parents to promote the achievement of individuation and autonomy. Rather, these findings indicate that adoptive parents are more likely to display child-rearing patterns that impair internalization and integration processes and, therefore, increase the risk of psychopathology characterized by disturbances of autonomy.

ADOLESCENTS' ADJUSTMENT AND MATERNAL INTERACTION PATTERNS

This study begins with the assumption that adoptees may be at increased risk for various psychological and academic problems due to complications inherent in adoptive parenthood. Hence, the study was designed to investigate four central aspects of adoptees' adjustment.

First, given that at least some adoptive parents fail to solve adoption-related problems and issues in a manner that is beneficial for their children, we expected adopted adolescents to appear less mature and to display more problems than nonadopted age-mates. By excluding "hard-to-place"children from the sample, the study extends previous research and allows us to see risks inherent in adoption.

Second, we proposed differences in adoptive and biological parent's child-rearing patterns. We used observations of maternal communication patterns to investigate these differences empirically as observations provide less biased information about child-rearing practices of parents than self-reports (e.g., Grotevant & McRoy, 1990). We expected adoptive moms to be less likely to express a sense of *connectedness* or *commitment to the child* when interacting with him or her (e.g., by initiating compromises and by agreeing with the child's suggestions). In addition, we assumed that adoptive mothers' interaction behavior would reflect a lower degree of *structure* (in terms of the frequency of maternal feedback and requests for actions) and *autonomy support* (e.g., evidenced by acknowledgments, questions, or indirect suggestions addressed to the child). Finally, we expected adoptive mothers to express a somewhat higher motivation to gain and keep the *control* over the interaction (e.g., by dominating the discourse qualitatively and quantitatively) compared to biological mothers.

Third, we examine the degree to which adoptees' problems—as perceived by themselves and by their mothers—are accounted for by differences in maternal interaction patterns reflecting the provision of autonomy support, structure, and involvement. We hypothesize that it is likely that adoptees' problems increase the more mothers tend to behave in a controlling manner (i.e., to dominate or control the discourse), while problems decrease the more mothers are able or willing to satisfy their children's need for self-determination (e.g., by providing opportunities for participation in decision-making), to provide structure (i.e., by offering feedback and requests for actions) and to promote a sense of relatedness (e.g., by initiating compromises).

Finally, we investigated the extent to which the developmental impact of specific maternal vocalizations are similar in adoptive and biological families. Although several studies on adoption elicited findings that parallel the role of parental caregiving characteristics in the development of nonadopted children, few researchers have addressed the question of similarities and differences in correlational patterns among adoptive and biological families.

Subjects

Subjects were recruited by asking official German adoption agencies to contact families with adopted children who were about 13 years old and who were not of a different race than the parents, foreign born, or "hard to place." Furthermore, the sample was limited to non-kin adoptions because they best represent the kind of family where the biological is separated from the social part of parenting.

A comparison sample of biological families with a 13-year-old child was also obtained (see Klein-Allermann, 1995). All families were predominantly from the lower to upper middle class. There were no differences between adopted and control families on background characteristics such as parents' marital status (all intact), age of the children, gender (60% of the adoptees and 65% of the nonadopted adolescents were females), or number of siblings (mean number = 1.17 for adoptees vs. 1.35 for controls). As expected, adoptive mothers were older and had been married for a longer time when they experienced the transition to parenthood. However, because demographic characteristics of adoptive parents have been shown to be unrelated to adoption adjustment (Festinger, 1990), we did not control for this.

In all, 52 adoptive and 43 biological families and their target children agreed to participate. The investigation began when the children reached puberty. Family discussions were available from the 48 adoptive and 34 biological families that comprise the sample for the following analyses.

Measures

Adolescents' *social, emotional* and *academic functioning* was measured using data from semi-structured interviews and a two-hour battery of tests administered to adolescents and mothers. Maternal perceptions of adjustment difficulties were assessed by asking mothers to rate the extent of their children's problems across different areas on a four-point Likert scale. Three scales (each containing three items) were derived from factor analyses and reflected the degree of *problems with peers* (α = .78), *school-related problems* (α = .78) and *emotional or self-related problems* (α = .68). Since all subscales were intercorrelated, an overall score was computed reflecting the extent of psychosocial problems in general (α = .82).

To assess the amount of *self-perceived problems*, adolescents completed several subscales of a self-report measure developed by Seiffge-Krenke (1984). The *overall problem score* (α = .91) reflects the degree to which adolescents rated themselves as having problems across five developmental areas (self, peers, school, future perspective, leisure time). Finally, we applied an instrument developed by Greenberger, Josselson, Knerr, and Knerr (1974) that measures the *psychosocial maturity* of adolescents (α = .91). High scores reflect mature work orientations, a strong sense of personal identity, and an internal locus of control.

Verbal interactions in mother–child dyads were evoked by applying the standardized "plan-something-together task."Conversations were audiotaped, transcribed verbatim, and coded using the coding system developed by Condon, Cooper and Grotevant (1984). Although that coding system is based on a model of relational functioning that focuses on four dimensions of individuation, we believe that it is a useful tool for examining communication patterns from the perspective of self-determination theory as well. Moreover, the three sets of exhaustive and mutually exclusive categories employed by this system allow coders to make judgments that require low levels of inference.

Before coding the conversation, each contribution was divided into codable chunks, or independent clauses, together with any dependent clauses that are connected to them. Next, each utterance was assigned a code category that best represented its function. Coders were trained to an initial agreement of 80 percent and were blind to adolescents' adjustment problems. All utterances were assigned to one of the three sets of code cate-

TABLE 1. Overview of Constructs, Behavioral Observation Categories and Examples

Dimensions of family context	Behavioral Observation Categories	Relational function	Examples
(1) Relatedness / Commitment			
readiness to dedicate time, attention, and resources to the child; expression of warmth, empathy, commitment, interest and involvement; affectionate and caring behavior without signs of overprotectiveness	Initiates Compromise (RESPONSE)	Compromises function to resolve disagreement about solutions to the task or about managing the task; sometimes function to appease disappointed participants	We can go to the Bahamas and then we can go to Paris. OK.
	Complies with Request for Action (RESPONSE)	Functions as an appropriate response to a request for action	Let's see, first day we'll fly to Rio.
	Disagrees / Challenges Other's Idea Directly* (RESPONSE)	Arguments for not accepting a particular suggestion; direct disagreements are explored by use of the first person singular pronoun	I don't want to go to Egypt. I think that would be boring.
	Disagrees... Indirectly* (RESPONSE)	Arguments for not accepting a particular suggestion; the speaker is already assuming an answer to the question	Isn't it awfully far? Do you think two weeks will be OK?
(2) Autonomy Support			
Direct Control (-)			
abstention from authoritarian discipline techniques, including pressuring language, attempts to gain control, expressed value for obedience and compliance, usage of power-assertive / punitive /coercive disciplinary strategies	Suggests Action or Location Directly* (MOVE)	Suggestions introduce an option of a location or activity for the vacation; a direct suggestion uses the personal pronouns I or ME to express the speaker's responsibility for the proposal. Include commands in the form of an imperative	I want to go to California. Check for the timetable.
	Relevant Comment* (OTHER)	Relevant Comments do not have a single definite function; RC's are coded if a remark does not exhibit one of the MOVE or RESPONSE functions	I've heard it's nice there.
	Length / No. Of Utterances*	Indicates dominance vs. shared responsibility	

Note: * these categories are inversely related to the main constructs of relatedness and autonomy support

continued

TABLE 1. (Continued)

Dimensions of family context	Behavioral Observation Categories	Relational function	Examples
Participation / Support for Self-Initialization			
supportive activities such as encouragement of self-initiated action and self-expression, provision of choice, acceptance of independent problem solving; assuming another's perspective or internal frame of reference; acknowledgment of the other's perceptions, acceptance of the other's feelings	Requests Information/ Validation (MOVE)	Seeks confirmation for a statement or seeks input that is pertinent to the accomplishment of the task; Requests are usually in the form of questions	All right? Do you want to learn to ski?
	Suggests Action or Location Indirectly (MOVE)	Indirect suggestions introduce an option of a location or activity for the vacation; usually indexed by the use of the first person plural pronouns	We could go to Yellowstone. How about flying to New York?
	Agrees With/Accept/ Incorp. Others' Ideas (RESPONSE)	Represents a "yes-vote" to someone's proposal of a location or activity	Good idea.
	Acknowledgment (RESPONSE)	Functions to affirm speaker's participation in the interaction	Hm, sure. / That's an idea.
	States Other's Feelings/ Mind Read (OTHER)	One person speaks for another person in the presence of that person and attributes to the other person ideas, desires, needs etc.	We will want to see the art museum.
Structure / Guidance	Answers Request for Information / Validation (RESPONSE)	Functions as appropriate responses to request for information / validation	It's not far. Yes.
provision of unambiguous contingencies, a meaningful rationale for requested activities and informational feedback or guidance concerning the child's agentic activity	Requests Action (MOVE)	Statements with managerial functions; they concern the procedures by which the group will accomplish the task	Wait a minute. Don't go so fast.

136

gories (Move, Response, and Other function). Table 1 lists the conceptual dimensions and the categories that indicated behavioral indices of concepts. The frequencies of each subjects' statements were computed and divided by the total number of utterances they produced to control for the different number of utterances occurring in individual mother–child dyads. Because of uneven distributions, all measures were also standardized using a z-transformation.

Results

Differences in psychological disturbances

Figure 1 indicates that adopted children describe themselves to be more likely to display problems compared to their nonadopted counterparts (see Figure 1). Adoptees scored lower on the maturity scale and slightly higher on the overall problem score compared to nonadopted controls. However, only the difference in maturity was significant ($t[68] = 1.95, p < .05$).

From the perspective of their mothers, adopted adolescents appear to be even more vulnerable. Significant differences were found with respect to emotional (self-related) problems ($t[92] = 2.11, p < .05$), family-related problems ($t[90] = 2.98, p < .01$), academic problems ($t[89] = 2.93, p < .01$), and the overall number of problems ($t[92] = 2.67, p < .01$). Adoptees' distinct vulnerability for learning difficulties is also reflected in their increased likelihood of being in the middle or low track of the German school system ($\chi_{[2]}2 = 10.34, p < .01$).

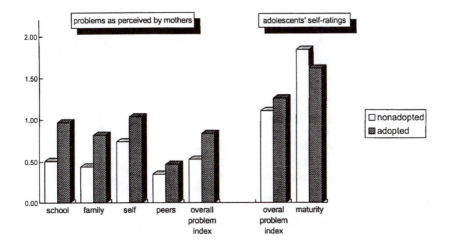

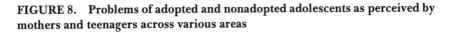

FIGURE 8. Problems of adopted and nonadopted adolescents as perceived by mothers and teenagers across various areas

Communication patterns of adoptive and biological mothers

Next, we hypothesized that adoptive mothers would be less likely to make statements that signal qualities of autonomy support, guidance, and involvement when interacting with their child than would biological mothers. Comparisons of biological and adoptive mothers' communication patterns (see Table 2) showed that, on average, adoptive mothers were less likely to initiate compromises and to comply with their child's requests. These differences indicate that adoptive mothers are less willing or able to create an atmosphere in which adoptees' need for relatedness is satisfied.

With respect to differences in maternal support of autonomy, results were mixed. As expected, adoptive mothers were more likely to dominate the discourse (mean number of utterances) and make fewer indirect suggestions than control mothers (see Table 2). At the same time, however, adoptive

TABLE 2.   Adjusted and z-standardized means for the behavioral observation categories for mothers from adoptive (AF) and biological (BF) families

Behavioral Observation Categories	AF (N = 48)		BF (N = 34)			
	Mean	SD	Mean	SD	t	P
(1) Relatedness / Commitment						
Initiates Compromise	-.21	.65	**.30**	1.30	2.13	p<.05
Complies with Request for Action	-.19	.53	**.27**	1.39	1.84	p<.10
Disagrees/Challenges Other's Idea Directly*	.13	1.01	-.19	.98	-1.42	n. s.
Disagrees... Indirectly*	.04	.83	-.06	1.21	-.42	n. s.
(2) Autonomy Support **Direct Control***						
Suggests Action or Location Directly*	-.20	.70	**.28**	1.27	2.01	p<.10
Relevant Comment*	-.08	1.02	.11	1.00	.84	n. s.
No. of Utterances*	**.26**	1.08	-.37	.74	-2.92	p<.01
Participation / Support for self-Initialization						
Requests Information / Validation	**.15**	1.06	-.22	.88	-1.69	p<.10
Suggests Action or Location Indirectly	-.17	.89	**.24**	1.11	1.84	p<.10
Agrees With / Incorporates Others' Ideas	-.05	1.00	.08	1.02	.59	n. s.
Acknowledgment	.10	1.07	-.14	.89	-1.04	n. s.
States Other's Feelings / Mind Read	-.07	.81	.10	1.22	.70	n. s.
Structure / Guidance						
Answers Request for Information/Validation	.09	.80	-.12	1.24	-.92	n. s.
Requests Action	.05	1.04	-.07	.96	-.54	n. s.

Note: * these categories are inversely related to the main constructs of relatedness and autonomy support mothers were less likely to make direct suggestions and were more likely to request information for validation of their perceptions.

Developmental impact of adoptive mothers' interaction patterns

Table 3 provides results concerning the relationship between maternal interaction patterns and adoptees' problems. We found that adoptees who had the fewest problems or the highest scores in the psychosocial maturity scale also had mothers who were more likely to acknowledge their child's statements, agree with the child's position, and initiate compromises. In addition, they were less likely to disagree directly or indirectly with their child's point of view or dominate the discourse (frequency of relevant comments). Finally, these mothers showed an increased tendency to state their child's feelings, offer indirect suggestions, and provide structure by making requests for action and responding to the child's questions.

Similarities and differences between adoptive and biological families

Since self-determination theory implicitly asserts that specific contextual factors facilitate or impair children's development in general, we expected similar correlational patterns in both subsamples. The results in Table 3 indicate that while the correlations are lower in general, most of the signs of coefficients for biological mother–child dyads are similar. Like their adopted counterparts, control teens with higher maturity scores and lower problem behavior scores were less likely to have mothers who dominated the discourse (here evidenced by the frequency of relevant comments) and who expressed their disagreement (at least directly) with their child's point of view. Moreover, control teenagers appeared to have fewer problems when their mothers acknowledged their statements and complied with their requests.

While these findings parallel those of the adopted adolescents, we also found evidence for differential effects. First, it appeared that the total number of mothers' utterances as well as mothers' compliances with the children's requests had no consistent relation to the measures of adoptive adolescents' adjustment while, surprisingly, nonadopted teenagers seem to be better adjusted when mothers dominate the discourse and refuse to comply. In contrast, mothers' readiness to disagree indirectly with their child's point of view had the expected positive relation only to adopted adolescents' self-reported problems. Second, while maternal readiness to respond to adolescents' questions was positively linked to adoptees' maturity, the opposite effect was found for biological mother–child dyads. Finally, while mothers' readiness to state their child's ideas or feelings seemed to be beneficial for adoptees, this tendency was related to nonadopted adolescents' problems.

TABLE 3. Bivariate Correlations between maternal communication patterns and indexes of adolescents' adjustment as perceived by adolescents and mothers

Behavioral Observation Categories	Adoptive Families (39 ≤ N ≤ 48)			Biological Families (29 ≤ N ≤ 34)		
	Maturity	Overall problem index (adol.)	Overall problem index (mothers)	Maturity	Overall problem index (adol.)	Overall problem index (mothers)
(1) Relatedness / Commitment						
Initiates Compromise	.15	-.25+	-.12	.11	.01	-.08
Complies with Request for Action	-.14	.35*	-.01	-.25+	.14	.44**
Disagrees / Challenges Other's Idea Directly*	.08	-.19	.21+	-.27+	-.02	-.12
Disagrees... indirectly*	.04	.05	.40**	.08	-.23	-.16
(2) Autonomy Support						
Direct Control						
Suggests Action or Location Directly*	-.12	-.17	.18	-.12	.20	.10
Relevant Comment*	-.17	.37**	.15	-.07	.09	.31*
Length (No. of Utterances)*	.06	.10	.07	.53**	-.01	.14
Participation/Support for self-Initialization						
Requests Information / Validation	-.10	.09	.02	.20	-.16	-.20
Suggests Action or Location Indirectly	.09	.00	-.20+	-.07	.18	-.20
Agrees With/Incorporates Others' Ideas	.21+	-.23+	-.04	-.28+	-.13	-.05
Acknowledgment	.28*	-.31*	-.10	.18	-.25+	.13
States Other's feelings/Mind Read	-.11	-.14	-.21+	-.05	.37*	.20
Structure / Guidance						
Answers Request for Information/Validation	.31*	-.15	-.19+	-.26+	.15	-.14
Requests Action	.22+	.11	-.21+	.16	-.08	-.12

Note. * these categories are inversely related to the main constructs of relatedness and autonomy support
+ p < .10; * p < .05; ** p < .01 (one-tailed)
Underlined pairs of correlations denote significant differences between biological and adoptive dyads for the categories indicated

DISCUSSION AND CONCLUSIONS

This chapter presented a study that compared family interaction and adjustment of adopted and nonadopted adolescents from the perspective of self-determination theory. Our results concerning differences between the adjustment of adopted and nonadopted adolescents indicate that, on average, adopted adolescents are less mature and more likely to display psychological and academic problems than are nonadopted adolescents, even though "hard-to-place"children were not included in the sample. Therefore, our results not only confirm previous findings (e.g., Bohman, 1980; Jungmann, 1987), but support our assumption that adopted adolescents' increased vulnerability can be viewed, at least in part, as a consequence of conditions or circumstances that are inherent in the adoption experience per se.

The findings relating to adoptive and biological mothers' interactive patterns provide evidence for the hypothesis that complications inherent in adoptive parenthood may reduce mothers' capacity to create an atmosphere in which adoptees may achieve a sense of belongingness. Our findings concerning adoptive mothers' support of autonomy, however, appeared puzzling at first. On the one hand, adoptive mothers seemed to be supporting autonomy insofar as they avoided controlling the discourse by offering direct suggestions and demonstrated their readiness to draw their children into the conversation by asking them for information and validating their opinions. These requests, however, were employed in a structure of asymmetrical discourse responsibility—as reflected in the mean number of maternal utterances—and were not employed along with indirect suggestions that would allow children to carry over the discourse either by picking up the mothers' ideas or by making their own suggestions.

Although we can only speculate at this point, we are inclined to interpret adoptive mothers' interactive style as rather withdrawn or restrained. On the surface, this style reflects frankness and interest in joint decision-making. However, it does not actually permit a mutual co-construction of the planning process because adoptees probably find it difficult to recognize—and, thus, to react to—their mothers' subtle attempts to direct the conversation.

The examination of linkages between mothers' interaction style and adolescents' degrees of problems indicated that maternal communication strategies employed in dyadic mother–child interactions explained some of the variance in both the adopted and nonadopted adolescents' adjustment. In line with self-determination theory, mothers' commitment—evidenced by an initiation of compromises—protected adoptees from experiences of conflict. In contrast, when mothers expressed differing perspectives, it seemed to aggravate adoptees' adjustment difficulties—presumably because maternal disagreement poses a threat to the child's striving for autonomy and competence, and it limits response options (see Zahaykevich, Sirey, & Spirk, 1987).

Evidence was found for the hypothesis that adoptees are more likely to achieve a strong sense of identity and display fewer problems in several developmental domains when their mothers' interaction style reflects a readiness to support self-determination by minimizing pressure or control, evidenced here by restricting the frequency of relevant comments. Adoptees were also better adjusted the more mothers provided structure in form of requests for actions and answers to the child's requests, as well as providing autonomy support in the form of indirect suggestions, acknowledging or agreeing with the child's initiatives, and stating the child's feelings.

Interestingly, we found, with only one exception, that significant correlations between behavioral observation categories and measures of *adoptees'* adjustment consistently showed the expected sign, whereas some correlations we found in *biological* mother–child dyads were the opposite of our predictions. Surprisingly, it seems to be beneficial for nonadopted adolescents' adjustment when mothers dominate conversation (evidenced by the mean number of utterances) and refuse to comply with their child's requests for action. In addition, nonadopted adolescents seem to be better adjusted the less mothers incorporate their child's feelings, agree with their child's remarks, or answer their child's questions. Given the paucity of research on families' communication patterns and adoptive family members' conversation styles in particular, it is too early to propose definitive conclusions; however, we offer three tentative interpretations.

First, unexpected linkages between observation categories and outcome variables may indicate that codes do not capture the psychological meaning of specific maternal speech acts in general. This explanation is not convincing because the behavioral categories in question had either no relation to measures of adoptees' adjustment or had the expected effect on adoptees' maturity and disturbances.

Second, as this study is cross-sectional, it does not permit causal inferences. Considering this limitation, a model positing bidirectional influences between adolescent development and qualities of maternal interaction patterns may be most appropriate for explaining the data. From this perspective, biological mothers' refusal to comply with and respond to the child's initiatives may be viewed as a reaction toward a less mature and "sociable" adolescent.

Although we need longitudinal data to clarify the direction of effects, we prefer a third interpretation which also emphasizes the "transactive" nature of discourse (Youniss, 1994). This explanation refers to the speed with which adopted and nonadopted teenagers negotiate developmental stages. Given that 13-year-old nonadopted adolescents are ready to individuate from parental authority and to demonstrate their tendency to deidealize parents by challenging their positions, biological mothers' may find it more necessary to deter their child from dominating the interaction. By elaborating their own point of view and by not complying with their child's requests or responding "eagerly"to them, biological mothers' may not only act for their own sake but may promote their children's development of self by eliciting rational and discursive self-reflection in adolescents (e.g., Hofer & Pikowsky, 1993).

This interpretation may initially seem to contradict central assumptions of self-determination theory; however, it does not when we keep in mind that the effect of mothers' parenting styles on children's adjustment is mediated by the way in which children experience their mothers' behavior (e.g., Deci & Ryan, 1994; Kreppner & Lerner, 1989). From this perspective, this study suggests that adopted adolescents are more likely to experience particular maternal reactions such as disagreements or "mind reading"as critical, judgmental, and controlling, rather than as informative and challenging, because they have a lower self-esteem and interpersonal trust than nonadopted agemates.

REFERENCES

Bohman, M. (1980). *Adoptivkinder und ihre Familien* [Adopted Children and Their Families]. Goettingen, Germany: Verlag fuer Medizinische Psychologie.

Bohman, M., & Sigvardsson, S. (1990). Outcome in adoption: Lessons from longitudinal studies. In D.M. Brodzinsky & M.S. Schechter (Eds.), *The Psychology of Adoption* (pp. 93–106). New York: Oxford University Press.

Bohman, T. M., McRoy, R. G., & Grotevant, H. D. (1993). *Acknowledging differences: A confirmatory test of the shared fate theory of parents' adaptation to adoption.* Paper presented at the biennial meeting of the Society for Research in Child Development, New Orleans.

Brodzinsky, D. M. (1990). A stress and coping model of adoption adjustment. In D. M. Brodzinsky & M.D. Schechter (Eds.), *The Psychology of Adoption* (pp. 3–24). New York: Oxford University Press.

Cadoret, R. J. (1990). Biologic perspective of adoptee adjustment. In D. M. Brodzinsky & M. D. Schechter (Eds.), *The Psychology of Adoption* (pp. 25–41). New York: Oxford University Press.

Condon, S. L. C., Cooper, C. R., & Grotevant, H. D. (1984). Manual for the analysis of family discourse. *Psychological Documents, 14,* 8.

Deci, E. L., & Ryan, R. M. (1994). Promoting self-determined education. *Scandinavian Journal of Educational Research, 3,* 3–14.

Deci, E. L., Eghrari, H., Patrick, B. C., & Leone, D. R. (1994). Faciliating internalization: The self-determination theory perspective. *Journal of Personality, 62,* 119–142.

Festinger, T. (1990). Adoption disruption: Rates and correlates. In D. M. Brodzinsky & M. D. Schechter (Eds.), *The Psychology of Adoption* (pp. 201–220). New York: Oxford University Press.

Greenberger, E., Josselson, R., Knerr, C., & Knerr, B. (1974). The measurement and structure of psychosocial maturity. *Journal of Youth and Adolescence, 4*, 127–143.

Grolnick, W.S., Deci, E.L. & Ryan, R.M. (in press). Internalization within the family: The self-determination theory. In J.E. Grusec & L. Kuczinsky (Eds.), *Parenting Strategies and Children's Internalization of Values: A Handbook of Theoretical and Research Perspectives.* New York: Wiley.

Grotevant, H. D., & McRoy, R. G. (1990). Adopted adolescents in residential treatment: The role of the family. In D. M. Brodzinsky & M. D. Schechter (Eds.), *The Psychology of Adoption* (pp. 167–186). New York: Oxford University Press.

Hofer, M., & Pikowsky, B. (1993). Validation of a category system for arguments in conflict discourse. *Argumentation, 2*, 135–148.

Hoffmann-Riem, C. (1984). *Das adoptierte Kind. Familienleben mit doppelter Elternschaft* [The Adopted Child: Family Life with Doubled Parenthood]. Muenchen, Germany: Wilhelm Fink.

Hoopes, J. L. (1982). *Prediction in child development: A longitudinal study of adoptive and nonadoptive families. The Delaware Family Study.* New York: Child Welfare League of America.

Jungmann, J. (1987). *Aufwachsen in der Adoptivfamilie* [Growing up in an Adoptive Family]. Weinheim, Germany: Juventa.

Kadushin, A. (1970). *Adopting Older Children.* New York: Columbia University Press.

Kaye, K. (1990). Acknowledgment or rejection of differences. In D. M. Brodzinsky & M. D. Schechter (Eds.), *The Psychology of Adoption* (pp. 121–143). New York: Oxford University Press.

Kirk, H. D. (1981). *Adoptive Kindship: A Modern Institution in Need of Reformation.* Toronto, Canada: Butterworth.

Klein-Allermann, E. (1992). Adoptierte Kinder und ihre Eltern: Familien eigener Art [Adopted Children and their Parents: Special families]. In M. Hofer, E. Klein-Allermann, & P. Noack (Eds.), *Familienbeziehungen* [Family Relationships] (pp. 250–265). Goettingen, Germany: Hogrefe.

Klein-Allermann, E. (1995). *Die Bewaeltigung jugendtypischer Entwicklungsaufgaben im Kontext der Familie* [Coping with Adolescent Developmental Tasks Within the Family Context]. Frankfurt, Germany: Peter Lang.

Knoll, K. D., & Rehn, M. L. (1984). *Adoption. Studie ueber den Adoptionserfolg und die psychosoziale Integration von Adoptierten* [Adoption: An Investigation Concerning Adoption Success and the Psychosocial Adjustment of Adoptees]. Nuernberg, Germany: Diakonisches Werk Bayern.

Kreppner, K., & Lerner, R. M. (Eds.). (1989). *Family Systems and Life-span Development.* Hillsdale, NJ: Erlbaum.

Merz, U. (1995). *Der Einfluss des Adoptionsvermittlungsprozesses auf die Entwicklung adoptierter Kinder und Jugendlicher* [Influences of factors accompanying the transformation to adoptive parenthood on the development of adopted children]. Unpublished diploma thesis, University of Mannheim.

Plomin, R. (1986). *Development, Genetics and Psychology.* Hillsdale, NJ: Erlbaum.

Ryan, R. M. (1995). Psychological needs and the faciliaton of integrative processes. *Journal of Personality, 63,* 397–427.

Ryan, R. M., & Solky, J. A. (1996). What is supportive about social support? In G. R. Pierce, B. R. Sarason, & I. G. Sarason (Eds.), *Handbook of Social Support and the Family* (pp. 249–267). New York: Plenum.

Ryan, R. M., Deci, E. L., & Grolnick, W. S. (1995). Autonomy, relatedness, and the self: Their relation to development and psychopathology. In D. Cichetti & D. J. Cohan (Eds.), *Developmental Psychopathology: Vol. 1* (pp. 618–655). New York: Wiley.

Scarr, S., & McCartney, K. (1983). How people make their own environments: A theory of genotype-environmental effects. *Child Development, 54,* 424–692.

Schechter, M. D. & Bertocci, D. (1990). The meaning of search. In D. M. Brodzinsky & M. D. Schechter (Eds.), *The Psychology of Adoption* (pp. 62–90). New York: Oxford University Press.

Seiffge-Krenke, I. (1984). Formen der Problembewaeltigung bei besonders belasteten Jugendlichen [Coping strategies used by stressed adolescents]. In E. Olbrich & E. Todt (Eds.), *Probleme des Jugendalters* [Problems in Adolescence] (pp. 353–385). Berlin, Germany: Springer.

Singer, L. M., Brodzinsky, D. M., & Braff, A. M. (1982). Children's belief about adoption: A developmental study. *Journal of Developmental Psychology, 3,* 285–294.

Sorosky, A. D., Baran, A., & Pannor, R. (1982). *Adoption.* Reinbek, Germany: Rowohlt.

Stanton, A. L. & Dunkel-Schetter, C. (Eds.), (1991). *Infertility: Perspectives from Stress and Coping Research.* New York: Plenum.

Wild, E. (1996, April). Variations in the quality of family climate, parenting style, and the psychosocial adjustment of adopted and nonadopted adolescents. Poster presented at the meeting of the Society for Research on Adolescence, Boston.

Youniss, J. (1994). *Soziale Konstruktion und psychische Entwicklung* [Social Construction and Development]. Frankfurt, Germany: Suhrkamp.

Youniss, J., & Smollar, J. (1985). *Adolescent Relations with Mothers, Fathers, and Friends.* Chicago: University of Chicago Press.

Zahaykevich, M., Sirey, J., & Spirk, M. (1987). *The construction of consensus in mother–daughter discourse.* Paper presented at the Meeting of the Society for Research in Child Development, Baltimore.

Chapter 9

The Meaning of Parent–Adolescent Interactions for Structuring Relationships and Society

Jeffrey A. McLellan
Catholic University of America

Miranda Yates
Menninger Foundation

The studies collected in this volume contribute to our knowledge of adolescent social development in a variety of ways. Each is most forthrightly grounded in individuation theory which examines interaction between adolescents and parents as an indicator of the status and quality of the relationship . However, the chapters also illuminate our understanding of the "interaction order" (Goffman, 1983) as worthy of study in its own right for what it tells us about social structure, its construction, and transformation.

Individuation theory posits a transformation of the unilateral relationship between parent and young child to a more bilateral or egalitarian relationship between parent and adolescent. The model for this transformed relationship is to be found in the reciprocity which has characterized friendship relationships throughout middle childhood and into the adolescent period. Youniss and his colleagues and Grotevant and his colleagues have elaborated on this theory of social development with studies supporting the general direction of the individuation transformation, but maintaining that the parent–adolescent relationship does not typically become as egalitarian as that between friends. Indeed, research using U.S. samples indicates that the distinct nature of the relationship between parent and offspring remains and that it varies between fathers and mothers and sons and daughters.

One of the main contributions of the authors in this volume is their use of direct observation and coding methods to examine individuation among Western European adolescents and their families. The concept of individuation was initially brought into the research mainstream by Grotevant and Cooper (1986) and their colleagues who directly studied the interactions of young U.S. adolescents and their parents. Most other studies in the area (e.g., Steinberg & Silverberg, 1986; Youniss & Smollar, 1985) relied upon interview or survey data. The present work recalls the original observational studies but has the advantage of the enriched conceptual work on individuation that has developed since. Given that interaction between parents and adolescents is at the heart of the concept of individuation, the work of these authors has been most fruitful.

The work of Hauser and Powers and their colleagues (Hauser et al, 1984) and Smetana (1988) also underpins and informs the studies in this volume. Hauser and Powers have looked at how parent–adolescent interaction enables or constrains adolescent ego development. In a longitudinal study they found that positive ego development in later adolescence was associated with earlier empathic and accepting interaction with parents. Smetana has focused on parent–adolescent conflict and found that conflictual interactions that take place in a supportive context promote the development of reasoning about personal choice and social convention.

The present work follows in the tradition of the U.S. studies cited above by informing theory through direct observation of interaction. In so doing, this work illuminate three major issues in the individuation process among young adolescents and their families. The first is the perseverance of parental authority in early and middle adolescence. The second is the increasing degree of interactional symmetry between adolescents and their parents. The third is the openness of the individuation process to variation based on factors from outside the immediate parent–adolescent interaction.

ISSUES OF PARENTAL AUTHORITY

The adolescents in the studies included here are relatively young. In the five studies that report upper age limits, three include no adolescents over 16 and none include adolescents over 18. Lower age limits range from 9 to 14 years. This youthfulness is reflected in the findings of the studies as they pertain to parental authority. This is most obvious in the study by Krappmann, Oswald, Schuster, and Youniss, which focuses on six mother–daughter dyads playing a competitive game. The daughters are pre- or young adolescents between the ages of 9 and 13. The authors present a strategic analysis of the daughters' attempts to win a game in the face of control efforts on the part of their mothers. Mothers took a fundamentally unilateral approach but generally employed indirect methods of control. Daughters generally resisted this approach through such strategies as challenging, ignoring, ridiculing, or ingratiating. However, there was some evidence, particularly from one dyad, of cooperation wherein the mother was sensitive to the daughter's demands and the daughter respectfully considered her mother's wishes. Overall, though, the relationships illuminated by the competitive situation were distinctly unilateral or untransformed from childhood. Given the relative youth of the daughters, this is to be expected based on individuation theory.

The chapter by Hofer and Sassenberg nicely illustrates the predominance of role (mother versus daughter) over task (to discuss hypothetical versus real issues) in determining the nature of discourse. Their data indicate a relative stability on the part of mothers and daughters within their roles, whether they are discussing a putative vacation or an actual point of conflict between them. As the authors put it, "Mothers gave structure to the interaction while daughters responded to or complemented their moves." This finding is in keeping with the U.S. studies of Youniss and Smollar (1985) showing that mothers are still not the same as friends, especially for younger adolescents.

Another example of parents holding to a position of authority is contained in the cross-sectional analysis of Noom and Dekovic. The authors report age-associated differences in the approach taken by Dutch parents with their younger adolescents whereby fathers disagree more with older adolescents than with younger adolescents. We could almost characterize this increase in disagreement on the part of fathers as compensatory for the propensity of mothers who appear to be acceding to demands of their adolescents by becoming more agreeable. An alternative interpretation is that fathers view older adolescents with seriousness because behavior at this age carries greater import both for immediate and long-term consequences.

ISSUES OF RELATIONAL SYMMETRY

Although the studies give us a portrayal of parents continuing to maintain authority over their adolescent children, they also give us a picture of emerging symmetry in the parent–adolescent relationship. For example, although the fathers in the Noom and Dekovic study disagree more with their offspring, as the adolescents get older, this seems to be in response to the fact that older adolescents are more active in discussions with parents, demanding more influence in decision-making.

Using two separate longitudinal samples, Noack and Kracke show somewhat different patterns for interactions between younger German adolescents and their parents. The adolescents were assessed when they were about 13 and 15 years of age; older adolescents and their parents were assessed when the youth were 15, 16, and 17 years. The early adolescence study indicates that parents become more directive of their offspring between the ages of 13 and 15, perhaps in response to the increased number of "conflictuous moves" on the part of the adolescents over this period. This finding is in keeping with the U.S. finding of an upswing in confrontational interactions between adolescents and their parents in mid-adolescence. A contrasting picture emerges from the authors' examination of interactions between older adolescents and their parents. Noack and Kracke hypothesized an increase in interactional symmetry between adolescents and their parents during later adolescence. As expected, the adolescents were more symmetrical with their parents in terms of issuing a similar level of directives and initiations of confrontation and, by the third observation, parents were less likely than previously to "mindread" (i.e., impute thoughts and emotions) for their adolescents. A limitation of the second study is that the coding scheme employed was not designed to assess affective expressions such as the "conflictuous moves" in the early adolescence study.

Kreppner and Ullrich present longitudinal findings of research on communication style following parents and children from when the children were approximately age 11. At the most recent data collection with adolescent sons and daughters aged about 15, the authors detect an increase in "negotiation" on the part of mothers and a decrease in "statements" which affirm one's position without considering the other's view. This follows an increase in "negotiation" and "statements" having taken place at age 13 on the part of adolescents in discussion with their mothers. Fathers use fewer "statements" with their children at age 11 and 12 than later, but negotiate more with adolescents over 13 years. Two differences characterize changes in communication patterns on the part of adolescents and fathers: more "silence" among 15-year-olds and less negotiation at age 13 than in earlier or later periods.

Although the focus of Buhl and Hofer is primarily methodological, it does inform the issue of relational symmetry between parents and adolescents. The authors seek to validate an approach that examines the relational propensities of adolescent females by presenting them with experimentally manipulated role-playing tasks. The tasks were hypothetical conflict situations between mothers and daughters. A main point to be taken from this study is the great importance of goal significance (i.e., the degree to which the hypothetical conflict is over the daughter trying to get something she really wants). Goal significance was the best predictor of stronger advocacy on the part of daughters such that those in the high goal significance condition initiated more arguments, more frequently weakened the mother's position, and were less likely to accept the mothers' arguments. Although the responses in the study are to initiatives on the part of a hypothetical mother, the study suggests that research looking at interaction between parents and adolescents should consider the degree to which conflict is over a topic that is particularly salient to the adolescent. Buhl and Hofer's study would indicate that adolescents would be more likely to attempt to achieve relational symmetry with parents over such topics than over relatively unimportant ones.

INTERACTION PATTERNS AND OTHER CHARACTERISTICS

Most of the studies in this volume go beyond describing interactional patterns pertinent to individuation and look for associations between such patterns and characteristics of adolescents and their families. Thus, we have Wild's study comparing families with adopted versus nonadopted young adolescents, Kreppner and Ullrich's examination of adolescents clustered according to ambivalence and dependence in their relationship with their parents, Noom and Dekovic's characterization of adolescents according to attitudinal, emotional, and functional autonomy; and Buhl and Hofer's experimental manipulation of goal significance.

Taken together, these findings indicate that patterns of adolescent–parent interaction are relatively permeable to the influences of family, relational, and personal factors. For example, Wild shows that interactions of 13-year-old adoptees with their mothers appear to be less clearly on the road to individuation than those of nonadoptees. Adoptive mothers are more generally unilateral in their approach to relations with their adolescents than nonadoptive mothers, being more likely to dominate the discourse and less willing to compromise with them. This finding may be partly a consequence of the propensity of these mothers to view them as less mature and more emotionally and academically troubled than nonadoptive mothers view their offspring.

Kreppner and Ullrich demonstrate that young adolescents previously characterized as "secure" (i.e., high on dependence and low on ambivalence toward their parents) interact with parents using a higher degree of agreement and nonverbal closeness to them. Another interesting influence on parent–adolescent interaction is the nature of interaction between parents themselves. The authors point out how the parents' mode of interaction with each other contributes to a pervasive family "communication culture."

Nevertheless, the nature of this culture appears to be complex and related to developmental change on the part of the adolescent such that mothers express more closeness than fathers at certain points and fathers more than mothers at other points.

The Buhl and Hofer research is unique among the studies presented here due to its experimental nature. An interesting contribution on their part is the salience of goal significance (i.e., the importance of how badly the adolescent is said to want what she is trying to achieve). In general, they find that higher goal significance contributes to a harsher interactional style in hypothetical situations characterized by arguing, "bad" atmosphere, and more negative reactions.

The sample of adolescents and parents studied by Noom and Dekovic is drawn from a larger survey sample. They employ the survey items to characterize the adolescents along three dimensions of autonomy: attitudinal, emotional, and functional. Their analyses reveal attitudinal autonomy (i.e., autonomy in areas such as goals, wishes, preferences, and values) as being the only significant correlate of interactional style among the three dimensions. More attitudinally autonomous adolescents tend to have more accommodating mothers, and to be more likely to negotiate with their mothers than with their fathers.

INTERACTION AND STRUCTURATION THEORY

Tesson and Youniss (1995) (see also Bigelow, Tesson, & Lewko, 1996) have recently articulated a theoretical perspective on development that emphasizes the importance of interaction routines. In part, this perspective derives from the structuration theory of Giddens (1987) who proposes that:

> Structure is both the medium and the outcome of the human activities which it recursively organizes. Institutions, or large-scale societies, have structural properties in virtue of the continuity of the actions of their component members. But those members of society are only able to carry out their day-to-day activities in virtue of their capability of instantiating those structural properties. (p. 61)

While Giddens is chiefly concerned with the manner in which broader societal structure is sustained and played out through micro-level interaction, the earlier work of Goffman (1967) and the more recent work by Tesson, Youniss, and their colleagues look to account for more proximate social structures such as personal roles and relationships. It is at this level that the studies contained in this volume make another important contribution.

The main point to be taken from this line of theorizing is that the routines of face-to-face interaction are constitutive of social structure. It is through patterns of interaction that roles and relationships are made real to those who possess and partake in them. Most importantly to adolescents and their families, it is through interaction that roles and relationships are transformed. Given the Western European and North American expectation of the teenage years as being a period for youth to begin gradually to take on adult status, the theory would predict that this structural shift would be manifested by and accomplished through routines of interaction between teenagers and salient others. Salient others could include peers, siblings, teachers, and bosses, but the present studies focus on interaction between adolescents and parents.

Individuation theory, as discussed above, points out that the task of individuation is really that of transforming the parent–child relationship and parent–child roles into something new. Structuration theory provides an account of how that transformation is instantiated. This is in contrast to a standard consideration of face-to-face interaction as being merely an indicator of the quality of the relationship between interactants. In the more standard approach, observation of interaction as a data gathering method is conceptually just another way of characterizing a relationship—it's not fundamentally different from the common North American method of asking parents and adolescents to complete rating scales that rate relationship quality scores such as closeness and conflict. Structuration theory goes beyond looking at interaction as an indicator of roles and relationships. Instead, it views interaction as the domain within which roles and relationships come into being, are actively sustained, and become transformed.

The authors of these chapters attend closely to a key feature of interaction that makes it capable of instantiating structure—its routinized nature. Without routines, interactants would constantly be in the position of constructing situational meaning afresh, as Tesson and Youniss state, "It is hard to imagine how persons would find the time to direct their interactions to the business at hand if they had to invent rules of interacting for each new event." The regularity or patterned nature of interaction is reflected in the ability of the authors to devise and employ coding schemes that represent communication styles, interaction strategies, and the like. An example is the Mannheim Argument Category System (MAKS) used by Hofer and Sassenberg and Buhl and Hofer which reflects the routinized nature of adolescent–parent discourse. MAKS reflects the organizing or structuring function of verbal routines as "initiatives," "reactions," and "arguments."

Great precision and effort went into the creation of the interactional coding schemes employed in these studies. These classifications of "slices of interaction" between adolescents and their parents may be seen as relationship quality indicators under individuation theory, but they may also be viewed as taxonomies of routines and strategies by which adolescents and their parents sustain and transform these relationships. For example, some routines used by daughters in Krappmann and colleagues' study appear to be oriented toward maintaining or reflecting the status quo in the relationship (i.e., cooperating, ingratiating) while others appear to be aimed at fostering change (i.e., thwarting, dominating). Structuration theory would view these routines as reflections of or manifestations from relational structure and as means by which the relationships are kept afloat or maintained. Most importantly from a developmental perspective, however, the theory can guide the study of the transformation of relational structure.

Giddens (1984) posits an elaborated definition of the concept of role as being a phenomenon of the "positioning" of actors. A social position is a social identity that carries a range of obligations and prerogatives. Social positioning is not static; it is constantly being enacted in face-to-face encounters as the actor goes through daily routines. Specifically, prerogatives are being exercised and obligations are being fulfilled. What is most important from the societal perspective is that the positioning of actors in their daily round is at the same time their "positioning within the broader regionalization of societal totalities" (p. 84) such as national, social class, gender, and age categories. In regard to age, Giddens points out that "positioning in the time–space paths of day-to-day life, for every individual, is also positioning within the life cycle or life path" (p. 85). The adolescents (and to a lesser extent the parents) in the present studies are seeking to reposition themselves in Giddens' sense or to renegotiate their relationships in the sense of individuation theory. This repositioning is both signified and accomplished through a shifting of prerogatives and obligations between adolescents and parents enacted through face-to-face encounters like the ones so carefully analyzed in this volume.

The theory and methods of interactional analysis are well employed in these studies as a means of understanding personal relationships. They may also be applied to the analysis of routines of interaction in their implications for higher-level societal structures. This application raises possibilities for further research. Specifically, we may ask how the patterns of interaction described in the studies are useful in preparing German youth for the society they are about to enter. This is an important question because German society, indeed the larger European society, is changing. The so-called welfare state constructed after World War II is being partially disassembled and reconceived. Germany itself is going through a massive adjustment as the East takes on Western democracy and capitalism and the West makes the massive expenditures associated with this change. In the midst of these changes, so too the family may be changing. Social class shifts may be occurring with more German youth delaying entry to the workforce and seeking college education. Simultaneously, German industrial production is changing following a general Western pattern of downsizing for greater efficiency. The present studies offer a conceptual framework and methodological approach to investigating adolescent's day-to-day interactions with important others, and they present the opportunity for us to assess how societal-level change is represented and constructed on the interpersonal level.

In conclusion, we observe that the studies in this volume make an important contribution by reporting details of parent–adolescent interactive exchange. In so doing, they put material substance on theoretical structures of individuation and structuration. They give detail to the term negotiation and bring to life the concept of transforming the parent–adolescent relationship through an array of observational methods. These studies show the similarities between Western European and U.S. families, thus giving generality to proposals in the theories of individuation and structuration.

REFERENCES

Bigelow, B. J., Tesson, G., & Lewko, J. H. (1996). *Learning the rules: The anatomy of children's relationships*. New York: Guilford.

Giddens, A. (1984). *The constitution of society: Outline of the theory of structuration*. Berkeley, CA: University of California Press.

Giddens, A. (1987). *Social theory and modern sociology*. Stanford, CA: Stanford University Press.

Goffman, E. (1967). *Interaction ritual: Essays on face-to-face behavior*. New York: Anchor Books. (Reprinted 1982 by Random House)

Goffman, E. (1983). The interaction order. *American Sociological Review, 48*, 1–17.

Grotevant, H., & Cooper, C. (1986). Individuation in family relationships: A perspective on individual differences in the development of identity and role-taking skill in adolescence. *Human Development, 28*, 82–100.

Hauser, S., Powers, S., Noam, G., Jacobson, A., Weiss, B., & Follansbee, D. (1984). Familial contexts of adolescent ego development. *Child Development, 55*, 195–213.

Smetana, J. (1988). Concepts of self and social convention: Adolescents' and parents' reasoning about hypothetical and actual family conflicts. In M. Gunnar (Ed.), *Twenty-first Minnesota Symposium on Child Psychology* (pp. 79–122). Hillsdale, NJ: Erlbaum.

Steinberg, L., & Silverberg, S. (1986). The vicissitudes of autonomy in early adolescence. *Child Development, 57*, 841–851.

Tesson, G., & Youniss, J. (1995). Bringing development and construction into sociology. In M. Ambert (Ed.), *Sociological Studies of Children* (Vol. 7, pp. 101–126). Greenwich, CT: JAI.

Youniss, J., & Smollar, J. (1985). *Adolescent Relations with Mothers, Fathers, and Friends*. Chicago: University of Chicago Press.

Author Index

Subject Index